CHELMSFORD
THROUGH THE AGES

BY GILBERT TORRY

EAST ANGLIAN MAGAZINE LIMITED IPSWICH SUFFOLK

£2·95

To Amelia Lavinia — in Memory.

I. S. B. N. 0 900227 26 5
Printed and published in England by
East Anglian Magazine Ltd
6 Great Colman Street
Ipswich, Suffolk.
©GILBERT TORRY, 1977
Cover design by Lynn Sheridan

CONTENTS

ILLUSTRATIONS

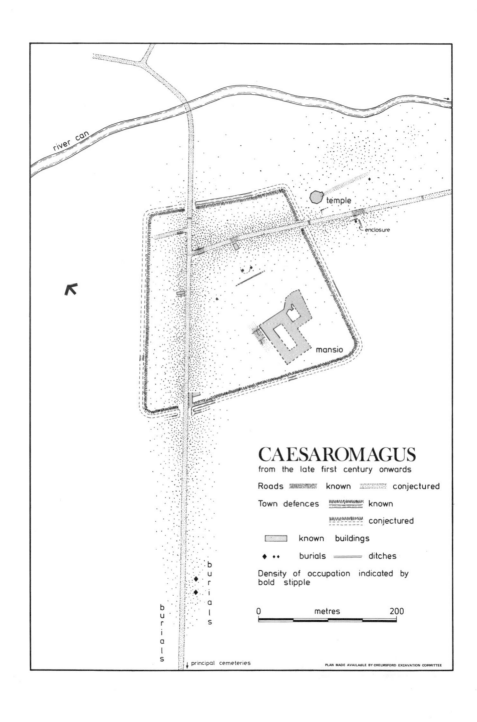

river can

temple

enclosure

mansio

CAESAROMAGUS

from the late first century onwards

Roads ▨▨▨ known ▨▨▨ conjectured

Town defences 〰〰〰 known

〰〰〰 conjectured

▭ known buildings

◆ •• burials ═══ ditches

Density of occupation indicated by
bold stipple

0   metres   200

b
u
r
i
a
l
s

b
u
r
i
a
l
s

↑ principal cemeteries

PLAN MADE AVAILABLE BY CHELMSFORD EXCAVATION COMMITTEE

CHAPTER I

THE ROMAN OCCUPATION

DURING the past 150 years the excavations of archaeologgists have revealed sufficient evidence of the existence of a rural settlement or a Roman town on the site now occupied as Chelmsford; it is unlikely, however, that the true origin of the town will ever be known, but it appears to have been some time between the departure of the Romans in A.D. 410 and the coming of the Conqueror. According to Camden, Chelmsford corresponds to the Roman station of Canœnium, but it is now generally supposed to be identical with Caesaromagus, a station in the direct road from London to Colchester.

If indeed it was not the veritable Roman Caesaromagus, it was undoubtedly a place of residence of some of those people. This is proved by the bricks, once forming part of a public Roman building, which were brought to light more than 100 years ago in the Moulsham area; further, in 1847 a Roman villa site was discovered in Mildmay Road, and the interim *Report of the Chelmsford Excavation Committee* reveals other finds; the diagram from this report is reproduced on the opposite page and shows the area and the position of the Mansion or lodging house lying between Orchard Street and Grove Road. Other examples of Roman occupation have also been found in Moulsham Street during the demolition of buildings in recent years.

There is no doubt that much more remains to be discovered about Caesaromagus, and a great deal of information could have been obtained during this and the preceding centuries when old buildings have been demolished, but whatever evidence may be in existence is at present covered by 19th and 20th century buildings, and there seems to be little scope for further useful excavations in the foreseeable future from this field, as most of the remaining buildings in the heart of Chelmsford comprise buildings of those two centuries which are likely to remain standing for several decades.

* * * * * * * *

The present town of Chelmsford stands at the confluence of the two rivers, the Chelmer and the Can, and derived its name from the former.

In some places in Domesday Book it is shown as Celmeresfort, in others as Celmeresforde. Other ancient records show the spelling as Chelmereforde, Chelmesford and Chelmsford. However, it is evidently a contraction of Chelmersford, all vehicles, cattle etc. 'being under the necessity of fording this river before bridges were thrown over it'.

Peter Muilman (in 1770) describes the town as having 'four streets, but is beautiful, regular, and well built. The entrance to it from the metropolis is over an old stone bridge, built by Maurice bishop of London (anno 1100) in the reign of Henry the First.' (It was replaced by the existing bridge in 1787.) 'No sooner is this passed over, than the attentive traveller is struck with the most agreeable surprize. A spacious ample street presents itself of a considerable length, in which are many handsome, good houses.

'At the upper end, upon a little ascent, stands the shire-house; which tho' no very magnificent building has a pleasing appearance. Over this is seen the tower, spire, and chief part of the church, which venerable structure terminates this little elegant piece of perspective. Each street lies with an easy descent towards the center, and is washed with a current of clear water. What contributes much to the peculiar cleanliness of this town, is it's being gravelled, and that with such skill and judgment as to form as it were a regular unjointed pavement.

'The sign posts which used formerly to project out so as to be a very glaring nuisance, are now entirely removed; and the inhabitants seem inspired with a laudable emulance in endeavouring to outvie each other in the neatness of their dwellings. The Chelmer and the Cann form here an angle; along which lie many pleasure gardens, &c. and some of them are agreeably laid out. On the banks of these rivers various temples and summer houses are built, some of which are so pretty in their construction as to display an elegance of taste in the projectors. In an open space (nearly a square) adjoining to the shire-house stands a conduit. When it was first erected is uncertain, as it bares no date, but it was beautified by the noble family of the Fitzwalters. It is of a quadrangular form about fifteen feet high, built with stone and brick; it has four pipes, one on each side, from which the purest water is perpetually flowing.'

From the time the Romans departed, little is known of the town's history, but by the reign of Edward the Confessor (1042-66) Chelmsford was in the possession of the Bishops of

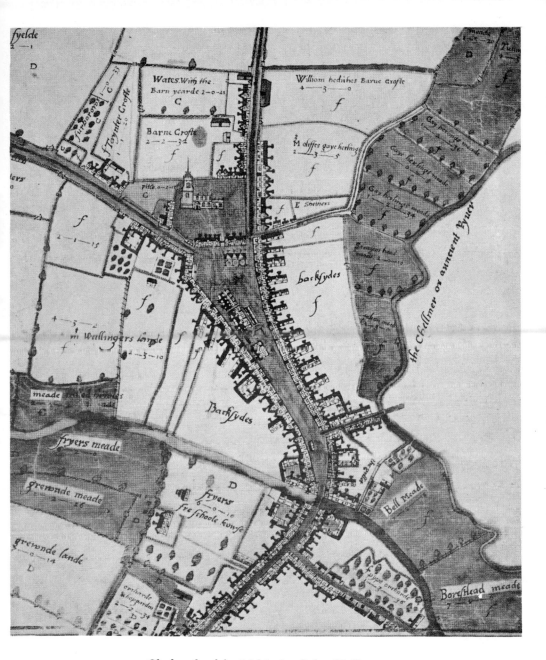

Chelmsford in 1591, by John Walker

9

The Coronation Festivities

1821, by Mary Hamilton

Waterhouse Lane c.1874

12

London and seems to have been of no particular importance until about the year 1100, in the reign of Henry I, when Bishop Maurice built the bridge over the river Can, that is, the bridge between High Street and Moulsham Street, adjoining Caters' Stores. This had the effect of bringing the route from London through Chelmsford across the bridge, whereas previously the public road to Braintree and other places to the north and north-east Essex to London led through Writtle, turning the corner at what is now Broomfield Road corner (the site of the Old Red Cow Inn) going on to Bayford Tye, and so to Margaretting.

From the time of the building of the bridge, the town began to rise in importance, and increased in the number of its houses and inhabitants, which was around 200.

At this time there does not appear to have been a market in the town, and the first Licence seems to be that which William de Sancta de Maria, Bishop of London, obtained from King John in the first year of his reign (1215); he also obtained a Licence for a Fair the following year.

The Chelmsford District Council Armorial Bearings

CHAPTER II

THE MANOR OF CHELMSFORD

THE PARISH of Chelmsford, otherwise Bishop's Hall, was divided from Moulsham, the other Manor in the Parish of Chelmsford, by the river Can; the main part of the town, therefore, lay in the Bishop's Hall Manor; part of the Manor of Bekeswell also lay in the Parish.

The Mansion House of Bishop's Hall is described as being on the north side of the town, near the river and the parsonage, about half a mile from the church, and continued in the possession of the Bishops of London until 3rd September 1545, when it was granted by Bishop Edmund Bonner to Henry VIII; the property continued in the Crown until 24th July 1563, when Queen Elizabeth granted the Manor and the Mansion House to Thomas Mildmay and his heirs for ever.

The Survey of 1591, however, records that in the reign of Edward III (1327-77) the Manor House was 'burnt and wasted with fire; before that it seems to have beene some ancient Baronye. This maner hath very faire demeane landes, woodes and wastes, and alsoe a great service viz. more than 200 tenantes, that holde of the same maner, their landes tenements and hereditaments by reasonable rentes, Customs & Services of which number above 30 are noble men, Knights Esquaires, & gentlemen of good countenance . . . . .'

Included with the Manor of Bishop's Hall granted by Queen Elizabeth to Thomas Mildmay was 'the Tollhouse to Keep Court in And All That Watermill called Bishop's Mill in Chelmsford aforesaid'.

The building known as Bishop's Hall has suffered a variety of changes and uses; as far back as 1836 Thomas Wright records that it had been in some degree modernized, and preserved in an excellent state of repair. Since then it has, in recent years, been used as a mill by Marriages. In pre-war days it was used as a canteen by Hoffmanns.

The present building, in Bishop's Hall Lane (leading from the bottom of Rectory Lane between the Hoffmann buildings towards Broomfield Fields) is in a very dilapitated condition. The description of its situation in the ancient records is sufficiently correct and immediately adjacent to the river Chelmer. A notice board offers it for sale; no doubt in due course it will find a buyer, but it is in a sorry state, and it is difficult to picture the building as the centre of feudal life of the times, the Lord of the Manor holding court, and having jurisdiction and control over the lives of the tenants on the Court Rolls. However, the records say it was then held in the possession of the ancient and honourable family of Mildmay, and, as there are no records of misdeeds, we may assume that the tenants had good reason so to regard the Lord and his family.

The family name, as is well known in Chelmsford, is preserved in 'Mildway Road', as well as in one of the 'Houses' at King Edward VI Grammar School, together with those of Tindal, Strutt and Holland.

Not far from Bishop's Hall, and a little to the west, was the Parsonage — a pleasant, rural mansion, surrounded by an orchard and garden grounds. There are, of course, no signs of the Parsonage now. (It was almost opposite the entrance to the cemetery).

At that time the road now known as Rectory Lane was Parsonage Lane; later the Parsonage was re-named the Rectory when it was occupied by the Rector.

The old locals refer to the Rectory as the Bishop's Palace but Chelmsford became the cathedral town of a new diocese in 1914 and John Edwin Watts-Ditchfield who was elected the first Bishop of the new diocese took up occupation of the mansion on the corner of Stump Lane in Springfield Road known as Bishop's Court, and successive bishops have resided there; it is, in fact, at present occupied by the Bishop of Chelmsford, the Right Rev. John Trillo. It would appear, therefore, that the Rectory was occupied by the Rector and not by the Bishop.

The mansion was demolished and the area used as a cricket field until the Marconi Company purchased the land and erected their factory and offices on it.

The entrance to the Parsonage or Rectory was the site of the garage entrance to No. 49 Rectory Lane, owned by Mr. Swain. His house was formerly two cottages built to house the gardener and groom employed at the Rectory; they were built in 1882, and the figures 1882 form part of the brickwork on the eastern wall of No. 49 Rectory Lane. The two cottages were converted into one house in 1912. There are some attractive mouldings forming part of the walls and a beautifully designed chimney stack was built to serve eight fire-places, four for each of the two cottages.

The sites of the houses immediately to the east of No. 49

15

Rectory Lane were stables belonging to the Rectory.

Bishop's Court was built in 1890 by the late Walter Ridley, of Ridley's Breweries; the cost of this magnificent mansion and 9 acres of land was £6000.

Amongst the graves in the cemetery in Rectory Lane is that of Carew Mildmay and St. John Mildmay, Archdeacon of Essex, Rector of Chelmsford, who died on 14th July 1878, aged 78; also in the same grave was buried his wife, Elizabeth Caroline, daughter of Lord Radstock, who died six months earlier on 6th January 1878, aged 79. Burials took place there as recently as 1950. Dr. Waller, who died on 27th April 1950, well-known in Chelmsford and greatly respected in the medical profession and by his patients is buried there; his wife is also in the same grave.

The Manor of Moulsham, or Mulsham, is referred to in many old records as 'Mulsho'.

Before the Norman Conquest it was in the possession of the Abbot and Convent of the Cathedral Church of St. Peter, Westminster, and continued vested in them until the Dissolution, when it shared the same fate as the rest, and came in course of time to the Crown.

On 23rd July 1540 King Henry VIII granted the Manor to Thomas Myldmay, Gentleman, one of the Auditors of the Court of Augmentations, for the valuable consideration of 20 years' purchase (£622.5s.8½d), together with a water mill with Mulsham Mill, and lands and woods on the Mulsham Fryth; and also all the messuages, mills, lands, tenements etc. in the parishes of 'Chelmesford, Mulsham, Great Badow, Stocke, Wydford and Writtle'.

The Mansion House stood on the left-hand side of the road leading to London, and was commonly known by the name of Moulsham Hall, 'Thomas Myldmay Esq., having obtained it, and converted it into the seat for himself and his posterity.'

It was rebuilt in the magnificent manner shown in the print on page 32 by Benjamin Earl Fitz-Walter, under the direction of Signor Leoni, the then famous architect.   .

Moulsham Hall was in the vicinity of the present Moulsham Lodge, possibly in a line east of Oaklands and the Rising Sun Public House in London Road.

Longstomps, or Long-stumps, is described as being between Moulsham Hall and Galleywood Common. In the field called 'Long-stumps' formerly stood a chapel which belonged to the Abbey of St. Osyth, as it was erected by that house. It was endowed with a great part of the tithes of Moulsham. Henry VIII, not long after the Suppression, granted, by his royal letters patent, 'the site of the chapel, with all its appurtenances, and the moiety of the tythes before-mentioned' to William Gernon. But Thomas Mildmay, marrying Avice, his daughter, the two families became united, and by such union the chapel and all that went with it were brought into the Mildmay family.

D.W. Coller in his *History of Essex* says 'the plough has long since passed over its (the Chapel's) foundation stone'. He pin-points the monastery institution 'at the footway leading to Galleywood Common'; this must have been at the point where Vicarage Road ended and the footpath (now Longstomps Avenue) began. The footpath existed in the 1920s before the area was developed, and began at the southern wall of Oaklands Park.

Peter Muilman also records that on the right hand side of the road that leads to the metropolis were six alms-houses 'which face the mansion of their late founder and their present benefactor'. They were founded by Sir Thomas Mildmay and his wife, Anne, for six poor people.

The road that led to the metropolis was, of course, Moulsham Street, and the Almshouses are still standing on the high ground in Moulsham Street opposite Braemar Avenue; a plaque is to be seen on the wall of the third Almshouse in the following words:

Founded by
THOMAS MILDMAY ESQ.,
of Moulsham Hall
1565
Rebuilt by
WILLIAM MILDMAY ESQ.,
of Moulsham Hall
1758

This confirms the situation of Moulsham Hall — approximately half-way between Moulsham Lodge and Moulsham School.

The Manor of Moulsham covered a very wide area, and included more than 1500 acres of Galleywood Common; also included was the house of the Black or Dominican Friars; little is recorded of this house, but the site on which it stood has for many years been known as The Friars or the Friers.

The future reports of the excavations by the Chelmsford Excavation Committee may prove very interesting reading.

Morant in his *History of Essex,* when referring to the Almshouses, says that 'Although they were founded by Sir Thomas Mildmay and his Wife, the sum they were endowed with had been granted by Sir Thomas's grandfather, Thomas Mildmay Esq., by his Will, wherein he gave twenty marks yearly out of his tythes of Tarling, to the masters, governors &c. of the free-school of Chelmsford' (the Grammar School).

£2 was to be devoted to finding an usher, whom the owner of Moulsham Hall would be entitled to nominate, and £6 would be divided, in equal proportions at Easter and Michaelmas, among the six oldest and poorest inhabitants. (In an admirable example of sex equality, three were to be men, and three women.)

£2 was to be spent on buying an ox or bullock for distribution to the poor of Moulsham on Christmas Eve; and £3.6s.8d. on three barrels of white herrings and four cades of red herrings for the needy in the first and second week of 'clean Lent'.

The Lord of the Manor also gave six tenements in Moulsham, settled in trust on the Bishop of London, for the use of six poor people, to be called 'Beadsfolks or Almespeople'. These Almshouses, standing too near the road, were taken down in 1758 'and rebuilt a little more back, and in a better manner than they were before, at the expense of William Mildmay, Esq., the (then) present worthy owner of Moulsham-hall'.

Moulsham has developed a great deal over the past 150 years, and the Survey of 1803 and 1804 made by Skinner, Dyke & Co. of Aldersgate Street, London, reflects the position.

Moulsham Hall together with the Mansion and Lands having an area of 24a.1r.26p. was in the occupation of the Government. There is no explanation for the Government's occupation, but it was at the time of the resumption of the war with France, and it may be that the area was taken over for purposes of defence; many forts and watchtowers were erected from Galleywood to Widford during the Napoleonic Wars.

Moulsham Lodge Farm was occupied by one John Marriage (a good, old-established Chelmsford name), having an area of 133 acres or thereabouts, who paid a yearly rent of £130 — under £1 an acre!

Moulsham Upper Stumps Farm, having an area of 14 acres approximately, was let at an annual rent of £15 to Thomas

Chandler. Thomas Chandler also was tenant of other parts of Moulsham Hall at similar rents.

Tile Kiln Farm was another farm in the Moulsham Hall area and was occupied by Edward Myhill. The area was 206 acres or thereabouts, but because he had been promised a lease he was paying an annual rent of £80.

Moulsham Meadow, partly in Moulsham and partly in Baddow was in the occupation of William Wall; 20 odd acres for £50 per annum.

Moulsham Street Farm, also occupied by William Wall, having an area of 53a.3r.4p., at a rent of £80.7s.0d. per annum, is recorded in the Survey.

All these farms were situated in the areas surrounding Moulsham Hall which, as I have said, stood approximately on the site of the present Moulsham Lodge.

Upper and Lower Stumps Farm covered a very large area, the western boundaries being on the main London Road which was then Moulsham Street and what is now Wood Street as far as the top of Longstomps Avenue where it joins Galleywood Road. The eastern boundaries of Upper and Lower Stumps Farms were on a line approximately with Longstomps Avenue: Upper Longstumps is, therefore, now covered by Bruce Grove, Campbell Close, Stewart Road and Hillside Grove, and part of the By-pass known as Princes Road. Lower Long Stumps extended as far north as St. John's Road and now comprises the whole complex of roads from Moulsham Street, beginning with Oaklands Park, Finchley and Rothesay Avenues, Braemar Avenue and Nursery Road, and as far eastwards as Oaklands Crescent, St. Vincent's Road, Moulsham Drive, and all those adjoining.

Wallace Crescent, the Isolation Hospital and eastwards to Beehive Lane were also part of the farmlands.

Lady Lane was named after Lady Mildmay; at that time the lane continued across Princes Road and into Moulsham Chase up to the Mansion House. The other end of the land appears to take in what is now Hamlet Road up to the point where it joins Moulsham Street.

* * * * * * * *

The Mildmay family is of very honourable and ancient standing; many of its members have, at different periods of our history, taken a leading part in the affairs of the state, and for more than 300 years it was connected by property and residence with the county of Essex. The house of Mildmay traces back its genealogy to the time of King Stephen, its first founder upon record, Hugh Mildeme or Mildme, flourishing as a person of considerable consequence in 1147.

During two or three succeeding centuries the descendants were seated in Lancashire and Gloucestershire, and in the early part of the 15th centrury the family became connected with Essex by the marriage of one of its members with the heiress of John Cornish, of Great Waltham. This lady was grandmother of Sir Thomas Mildmay, who appears to have stood high in the favour of Henry VIII, under whom he held the office of Auditor of the Court of Augmentations at the time of the Suppression of the religious houses and, like others about the throne at that period, he was enabled, partly by purchase and partly by grant, to build up a family estate in Essex from a portion of the spoils.

His four sons became the heads of great families. Thomas the elder, settled at Moulsham Hall; and his son, by marriage with the only daughter of Henry Ratcliffe, Earl of Sussex, brought the claim and title of the barony of Fitzwalter into the family. This branch, however, became extinct in 1756, on the death of the last Earl Fitzwalter. William, the second son, who resided at Springfield Barnes, succeeding to the estates, became seated at Moulsham Hall. Sir Walter Mildmay, the fourth son of Sir Thomas, acquired Bishop's Hall and Moulsham. He founded Emanuel College, Cambridge, and was Chancellor of the Exchequer and one of the Privy Council of Queen Elizabeth.

Sir Thomas Mildmay gave to Sir Humphrey Mildmay, one of his sons who held the high post of ambassador of France, the estate of Danbury Place. But the next heir, dying without issue, devised it to his wife, who married again, to Dr. Cory; they had a daughter, who on her marriage carried the palace of the Lord Bishop of Rochester from the family of Mildmay to that of Ffytch.

Sir Henry Mildmay, Knight, was Master of the Jewel Office in the time of Charles I.

In the conflicts of the succeeding reign, and the turmoils of the Commonwealth, the house of Mildmay was divided against itself; one of them, becoming a fierce republican, and bringing down upon his name the dark stain of regicide; while the other dared and endured much in support of the royal cause.

Perhaps to the misdeeds and the losses and changes of that day may partly be attributed the withering of the numerous family offshoots which once flourished in the Essex soil. Indeed, so largely had this family grown in wealth and honours, that about 1620 there were nine distinct branches settled in this county, the baronet, as the head, being followed by a goodly array of seven knights. These were Sir Thomas Mildmay, of Moulsham Hall, Bart., Sir Henry Mildmay, of Woodham Walter, Knt., Sir Humphrey Mildmay, of Danbury, Knt., Sir Henry Mildmay, of Wansted, Knt., Sir Thomas Mildmay, of Springfield Barns, Knt., Sir Henry Mildmay, of Graces, Knt., Sir Walter Mildmay, of Great Baddow, Knt., Carew Harvey Mildmay, Esq., of Marks, and Sir Robert Mildmay, of Terling, Knt.,

All these branches have long disappeared. Some have died away, others have been united by marriage, or lopped off and removed elsewhere. But the noble trunk, with the Paulet branch engrafted on it, remained rooted in the soil of its olden manors of Moulsham and Chelmsford. Carew Harvey Mildmay, the last of the line, left his entire fortune to his grand niece, Jane Mildmay, mother of Sir Henry and the then Rector of Chelmsford. This lady, in 1786, married Sir Henry Paulet St. John — the grandfather of the then baronet, who in 1790 assumed the surname and the arms of Mildmay.

Moulsham Mill, opposite Goldlay Avenue, was at that time let at £112 a year. It was then in the occupation of Abraham Bullen on a lease for 21 years from Michaelmas 1792.

The map attached to the Survey of 1803 shows a hop field on the southern side of Baddow Road. It was quite a size, having an area of more than 11 acres. It covered an area from Manor Road eastwards to the eastern end of Wallace Crescent and south in a line with Goldlay Gardens. There were a number of hop gardens in the town, mainly east of the High Street and north of Springfield Road — possibly connected with Gray & Sons' Brewery.

The Windmill Public House, the main entrance of which was in Moulsham Street (demolished during the recent development of the Ring Road) and the back entrance in Baddow Road opposite the Regent Theatre, 'with stabling, outbuildings and Yard and Way into Badow Lane', was the subject of a lease granted for 27 years from Michaelmas 1794 at £19.10s.0d. per annum. There was a hop garden quite near to the south east of this public house, and may have been in some way connected

21

with it.

The Survey contains further details of the whole area and contains items of considerable interest to anyone particularly concerned with statistics, but the foregoing descriptions will give the reader a general idea of the outline of the greater part of Moulsham in the beginning of the 19th century. The map shows no buildings beyond the point where Grove Road joins Moulsham Street, although there were, of course, the six Almshouses opposite the point where Braemer Avenue meets Moulsham Street, as I have already mentioned.

The area from Hamlet Road to Hall Street on the eastern side of Moulsham Street and extending eastwards to Mildmay Road was another hop garden of more than 10 acres. All the land east of Moulsham Street as far as Beehive Lane area was open fields.

Mildmay Coat of Arms: Argent 3 lions rampant azure armed and langued.

CHAPTER III

THE 16th CENTURY

THE MAP of Chelmsford in the year 1591 annexed to the Survey of that year is a remarkable work of art; a copy is reproduced on page

The Cathedral, then known as the Parish Church of Chelmsford, is the dominating edifice at the northern end of the High Road, which was then referred to merely as 'the King's highway'; the Survey records that one Jonas Carsey owned one tyled stall, free parcell of two stalles tyled under one roofe, lying between the lane called Shoprowe Lane alias Potters Lane on the one part and the King's high way leading from the Church to the Stone Bridge . . . . .'.

As the row of buildings running north to south on the King's highway (approximately from what is now the site of Crown Passage to London Road corner), was known as 'Middle Row', Potters Lane must have been on the opposite side of the road, and occupied the area from Westminster Bank to Grippers, the Ironmongers.

South of the Cathedral and the churchyard surrounding it was a row of buildings approximately in the position of the present Shire Hall. These buildings in 1591 are described in the Survey as 'Newe against the Churchyarde'. One of them occupied by Thomas Standish was a tenement 'at the east end of the Churchyarde abutting south upon the Markett Crosse of Chelmsford and north upon the Churchyarde and West upon the Tolhouse or Courthouse of Chelmsford'. Markett Crosse is the building shown on the Survey's map of Chelmsford standing upon four pillars in the middle of the road approximately opposite Barclay's Bank. In 1591 it appears to have been occupied by one John Ryson, for the records say: 'John Ryson holdeth the building called the Markett Crosse of Chelmsford situate in the open market called the Cattle Markett and the Corne Markett and for the moste parte used of the Cornmen.'

The whole area in front of the Tolhouse or Courthouse on each side of the highway from Tindal Square on the one side and Waterloo Lane on the other as far along as the Chelmsford Co-operative Stores appears to have been an open market of stalls, some 'tyled', others open. Parts of the market were known as Butchers Row, the Fishe Market and the Corne Market, and Potters Row, all on the western side of the highway.

23

On the same side of the highway, Thomas Mildmay is described as being in occupation of waste land 'Before the Crane'. The Crane was a public house and, no doubt, on or near the site of Crane Court.

The building known as Markett Crosse must have been an imposing looking building. It is described as 'A faire building called the Markett Crosse or Session House verie convenient and necessary for the Justices themselves, their under-officers and ministers and alsoe for all sortes of subjects to be attendant there, as well as for the common Gaole and prysoners soe as all may commodiously serve at their convenient ease in the same'.

Morant in Volume II of his *History of Essex* says 'Executions usually took place in olden times at Markett Crosse'.

On page 7 of the Survey it records that 'The Lorde's bayliff of the Manor of Chelmsford gathereth up and answereth to the Lorde of the Manor the profits of the ffaire holden yerely on May daye with the commodities in the standings for upholsters, brasiers and pewterers, and all other kinds of artificers using the same at the time of the said faire.'

Two fairs were held annually, the first on 12th May and the other on 12th November. There was also a Wool Fair in the latter part of June annually.

* * * * * * * *

Although the building known as Markett Crosse is shown in isolation in the Map of Chelmsford in 1591, there were buildings adjoining thereto. One William Pamplyn is recorded in the Survey as occupying 'one tenement called "Curdes" abutting west upon the tenement nowe of Richard George, and east upon the Churchyard Gate next to the Crosse . . . .'. Thomas Standysh, as I have already said, had a tenement abutting on the north of the Crosse. There were also houses situate behind the Shire House as well as shops, but these are not, of course, to be seen in the map. There was also an inn called the Red Cross behind the Shire House; all these are described as being 'by the Churchyard'.

The row of houses lying along the north eastern corner of the churchyard is Church Street or Brockhole Lane; these were of freehold tenure and occupied in some cases by the freeholders and others by tenants. The Survey records that William Clarke, Gentleman, 'holdeth one messuage, garden &c. called Josephes lying between the tenement of Thomas Wallenger

24

gentleman on the one part and one tenement called Mayes on the other part'. As the freeholders are referred to as 'gentlemen', we may conclude that the tenements were of good standard and better, for example, than the houses next described which were described as 'Almose housen, one in the occupation of Luke Whale thother in the occupation of William Springfield. Whales tenement abutteth south upon the tenement of Quenes now in the tenure of William Atkyns Thother abutteth south east upon the tenement of John Webb and west upon the tenement of Thomas Skott. theis are Almoshouses by suffrance not having any graunt to warrant them from the prince or lorde of the manor for the mortizing of them'.

John Webb was the freeholder of another of the tenements 'abutting south east upon thaleshouses now in the occupation of (the said) Luke Whale and west upon the tenement of Thomas Skott'.

This part of the Survey gives further details of other adjoining tenements and their occupants, including one tenement called 'The Chequer'. This sounds like an inn, and it may have been, although not described as such. But it must be remembered that houses and other buildings were not numbered then as they are nowadays; most of the buildings were identified by names and signs. And if you were to study the Survey you would find many buildings in High Street or the King's highway with such names and descriptions that you would be forgiven if you concluded they were all inns; they may have been, but not necessarily so. However, with Chelmsford as it is on the main highway between London and the coast, it is not surprising to find a large number of inns.

The Survey, under the heading which comprises details of the buildings I have just described, records also that Richard Nycolls gent 'holdeth one messuage &c. called the Maltingshouse in the tenure of John Hall'. This is quite likely the Malthouse, part of the capital messuage known as Guy Harlings or Herlings in New Street as it adjoined on the south side a building and piece of land once belonging to Robert Paperett, Brewer.

This was doubtless the Lamb referred to in White's *History of Essex*. The Survey refers to this building, then held by John Wrighte being 'one messuage and curtilage abutting south upon the lane leading down to Tunman Mead (now the Car Park) and north upon the tenement called the Lambe and west upon the street called Newstreete by fealtie suit of court and the yerely rent of one Redd Rose payable yerely at the feeste daye of St. John the Baptist'. You will notice that 'the Lambe' is not described as an inn.

An interesting point arises in this description in referring to the rent of 'one Redd Rose'. There are a number of buildings in the country in respect of which the rent payable is one red rose. The origin of this goes back to the 14th century and Sir Robert Knollys, close friend of Edward the Black Prince and renowned leader of the English Free Companies in the French Wars. After his return to London in 1346 he bought two small houses opposite each other in Seething Lane in the City of London.

To connect the two houses across the narrow lane an Haut Pas, or foot-bridge, was built across the lane. This was a misdemeanour as no sanction had been obtained from the civic authorities. In other words, he had not obtained Planning Permission! Guildhall, through the Common Court (or Common Council), took a lenient view of the offence but fined the offender.

The City Fathers decided that Sir Robert Knollys should present himself annually to the Lord Mayor to pay the fine. This consisted of a red rose, 'fresh pluck't' every Midsummer Day from his garden in Seething Lane, to be presented as a tribute to the first citizen of the City of London. Sir Robert did this every year until old age and infirmity prevented him from doing so.

This ancient custom was allowed to lapse for a time, but it is now observed annually at the Mansion House on June 24th, when the churchwardens of the Church of All Hallows place a red rose on the altar cushion and take it in procession up the stairs of the Mansion House to the Lord Mayor. The late Rev. P.B. Clayton, ('Tubby' Clayton), vicar of All Hallows, revived the ancient custom in 1924. The rent of a red rose is virtually a peppercorn rent and originally associated with a bridge, and there are instances in the records of properties in the City of London evidencing this. One of these properties is situate in the Ward of Queenhithe, south of Mansion House Underground Station; the bridge has long since disappeared but lay between Queenhithe Dock (the only remaining Saxon Dock in the country), and Brooks Wharf upon which the Samuel Pepys Hotel is built. There are other instances — one was the subject of the Case of 'Foljambe v Smith's Tadcaster Brewery Co.' in the Chancery Division of the High Court in the year 1904, which found for the Plaintiffs, who were able to prove that the property was subject to the payment of one red rose and that the notice to quit was properly given.

In view of the origin of the red rose rent I am inclined to the conclusion that the rent of one red rose payable in respect of the tenement in New Street indicates that a bridge was in existence there, and the following entry in the Survey rather bears this out for it records: 'But by one entry made in the Court Roll Anno Septimus Henrici Octavi it appereth that the said redd rose was to be paid for a way in forbarslane leading to Springfield Mill containing in length XI perches and in breadth XI foote.'

Before the Car Park was built, the level of the ground was around 10 feet lower than at present. The eastern wall surrounding Guy Harlings abuts upon the footpath adjoining the Car Park, which lies between Guy Harlings and Springfield Mill, and no doubt a bridge was in existence even at that time.

* * * * * * * *

'The Lambe' was held by one William Sheather, and is described as being 'a messuage with divers buildings, altogether called Manningtreys alias Battens And the said two messuages called Manningtreys abutteth upon the tenement called The Lambe on the south part, and upon the Capital messuage and faire place called Guy Herlings or Guy Harlings, so named from an ancient Norman possessor of it, Guy de Harling, with divers buildings &c. with one large room called the Maltinge House, divers yeardes, gardens, curtilages, orchardes and waters, and parcels of grounde, on the backside sometime of Thomas Duke'. This property is sufficiently near Duke Street to lend an explanation to the name of that street.

North of Guy Harlings was a range of orchards belonging to Ann Wigglesworth, William Hedyche and William Broadbarnes. William Hedyche held 'one Grange or barn of 5 acres called Arrowsmethes abutting north upon a parcel of the demesnes called Broomfeild'. Ann Wigglesworth's orchards and buildings bordered on Guy Harlings' and north upon William Hedyche's property. The orchards were between Guy Harlings and the new Police Station on the corner of Victoria Road and New Street.

There were no buildings beyond this point until Bishop's Hall was reached. The site of Bishop's Hall is (as mentioned earlier) in a very dilapidated condition, and a notice offering it for sale has been attached to it for some time.

It would appear that there were houses between those abutting upon New Street and the site of the Car Park adjoining the Swimming Bath at the bottom of Waterloo Lane, and evidence of this is contained in the entry in the Survey relating to property owned by Thomas Mildmay armiger 'One tenement some time of Thomas Rooper abutting west upon the house called the Vicaridge or Priests House and east upon the tenement nowe of William Sheather'.

* * * * * * * *

The Survey does not appear to include reference to all the buildings shown on the map: for example, the buildings shown along the western side of the Cathedral between the site of W.G. Webber's, the Jewellers, and the Cathedral Hall. However, let us now take a look at the western side of High Street; this is the row of buildings approximately from Crown Passage to London Road corner. Starting at the northern end, the first building was known as 'the Rammes', occupied by Thomas Arnott. The Rammes is described as being in Middle Row and abutting south upon the tenement of John Pampley called 'Copthall' and north upon the customary tenement of John Wharton, then of John Munnes. A 'customary tenement' was the term used in respect of property held according to the custom of the Manor, a class of ownership between freeholders and villeins. Customary freeholds were found in some manors, principally those of ancient demesne.

John Pampley's tenement abutted south upon the Newe Shambles; he also owned another adjoining tenement (later 'dismembered and made a shambles') to the north of the Three Tonnes and south of the tenement of Christopher Nashe. The Three Tonnes or Three Tuns would have been approximately on the site of Crown Passage.

South of the Three Tuns was the tenement occupied by Thomas Purkyn; south of Thomas Purkyn lived one Thomas Watson, and John Wright (possibly the same man who occupied the tenement on the northern corner of Tunman Mead Lane (Waterloo Lane) occupied the last tenement of Middle Rowe (approximately opposite the corner of London Road).

28

St. Mary's Church, Chelmsford c.1770

The Post Office at the Black Boy Inn, 1762

29

The High Street, look

towards the Shire Hall

The Old County Gaol, c.1810

Moulsham Hall

Before London Road was widened and the shopping precinct developed, the Half Moon Inn stood on the corner of London Road; the Half Moon is shown on the photograph on page 90 and would have stood approximately in the middle of the road on the sign 'No Entry'.

When the Half Moon was demolished (between 1900 and 1901), the site was converted into shops, one a greengrocer's and the other a fishmonger's.

Just beyond the doorway of the Half Moon is shown the doorway of the old Salt Hall, much in use when salt was a bonded article and sold for a guinea a bushel. An archway visible down the narrow passage beside the shop shows where the old salt bins stood.

In later years a public convenience was built on the site of the pavement shown in front of the tall building which for many years was occupied by Norwich Union Insurance Society.

These buildings, at the time of the Survey, were the site of John Wrighte and his two adjoining neighbours to the north of him, Thomas Free and John Eve; John Eve's tenement was called 'Samptons'. North of 'Samptons' was a tenement belonging to the Guild of Corpus Christi.

From the descriptions of the tenements forming Middle Rowe and from a look at the map you will see that the highway must have been fairly narrow; the surfaces of the roads at that time were gravelled.

Now let us have a look at the other side of the street from the Stone Bridge opposite Caters.

If you look at the map you will see the river Can running west to east with the 'Fryers' and pype orcharde on the south and backsydes and Bell Meade and Boreshead meade on the north.

The large building on the south-eastern corner of Backsydes which is also the northern side of the river was the Lion Inn, held by Sir John Petre, knighte. It is described as a 'cupital measuage or inn with one cartwaye, and one other tenement annexed to the same sometime called the White Harte, abutting uppon the river and the tenement of Sabrett'. Sabrett's tenement is the building in the immediate south-eastern corner of Backsydes, immediately opposite Caters, which is now a Chemists, 'Chemimart'. Doubtless it has changed hands many times since 1591 and had many a change of use. However, from the year 1870 it was occupied by Nickols & Jefferies, Cheap Hatters & Outfitters, until 1965 when it was demolished.

An interesting article written by my old friend, Lionel Hills, is contained in the December 1975 issue of *Essex Countryside* in which he says that in 1915 he started work at that establishment at the age of 12½; the day's work began at 8 a.m. and finished at 8 p.m. The farmer could buy a square crown stiff hat, and caps priced from 1/6d., and a black bowler hat for 3/9d. A photograph of the shop is reproduced on page 34 of the *Essex Countryside*, and part of the balustrade of the stone bridge can be seen in the left-hand corner of the photograph. By kind permission of Mr. Hills I am able to include a copy of the photograph on page 49

The White Harte, then, was the building immediately west of Nickols & Jeffries' building. Next to Nickols & Jeffries building was Mary's tenement abutting south upon the Lion, which in turn adjoined the tenement of Thomas Hawes. Next door was an apothecary. Thomas Hawes' tenement was known as 'Sharpes' or 'The Grange', and may have been quite a sizeable building.

Bearing in mind that the Chemists now on the other side of the Stone Bridge is Body's, it is a curious coincidence that the name of the apothecary was Thomasine Bodye!

A number of tenements, notably 'Wymonds' and another called 'Chaundlers', both large buildings from the descriptions in the Survey, divided Thomasine Bodye's from the Inn called the 'Black Boy', which stood on the site at present occupied by Baxters. This inn is not to be confused with the inn, the 'Old Black Boy', later built on the site of the 'Crown Inn' on the opposite side of the High Street and shown on the print of the High Street by J. Ryland in 1762. (See page 29 .)

The High Street at that point was quite a wide thoroughfare but narrowed further north between what is now London Road corner and Crown Passage; this part of the street has not been widened to any extent since then. Many an accident has occurred there caused by congestion of traffic within such narrow confines; and when cattle were permitted to be driven through the town, accident hazards were greater. In the 1920's and 1930's great was the chaos, particularly around mid-day when scores of cyclists leaving Hoffmans and Marconi's rode through the town on their way home to a quick meal and then back again by 1 o'clock. No canteens at the works in those days!

On Market Days the High Street was best avoided when cattle were being driven through to the market which was then held in Market Road on the site now occupied by the Retail Market and the multi-storey car park. It was worse on a wet day when the street was filled with shoppers from the villages as well as Chelmsfordians doing their local shopping, and vehicles; the animals would plunge and slip and fall on the greasy surface of the street, and often on to the pavements. Mothers rushed their children into the shops to avoid the danger of sliding hooves and flaying horns. Add to this an Eastern National 'bus moving slowly along amidst the cyclists, and you have a pretty gloomy picture of the High Street at that time.

* * * * * * * *

Beyond the Black Boy, going towards London Road corner, were a large number of inns, all bearing their inn signs.

A tenement then belonging to the Corpus Christie Guilde of Chelmsford separated Chaundlers from the 'Dolphin', adjoining which was a tenement called 'Sharpearrows'; then the 'Rose Inn', next to which was the 'Beare Inn'. The Survey then records that, next to the Beare, 'T. Munke holdeth one capitall messuage and divers edifices late called "The Bull".' Somewhere along the line of buildings was an Inn called the 'Robin Hood' but I have been unable to pinpoint it. There was also a Brewhouse tucked in somewhere between Sharpearrows and The Beare. (Later there was another 'Dolphin' inn in Back Street).

Before leaving the High Street, some entries in the Survey record that Ann Bridges, widow, owned or occupied a tenement called the Corner House at Colchester Lane; Colchester Lane was the name of Springfield Road at that time, and Widow Bridges' tenement was on the south east corner, until recently occupied by Collins & Son's China shop but now by Dorothy Perkins. Next to the Corner House was the Bores Head Inn, and adjoining it on the south, that is, towards Moulsham, was Smythes forge, abutting south upon the tenement of Widow Clarke. This is the only forge I have found recorded so far, but there appear to be a number of widows!

As I have already mentioned the Newe Inn stood on the opposite corner of Springfield Road (formerly occupied by Boots the Chemists); and adjoining it in Springfield Road was a tenement and stables and garden, and four other houses, the fourth one described as 'adjoining the bridgefoote' which indicates that the four tenements must have been of considerable size. An interesting fact emerges from the records, which describe one messuage in Colchester Lane 'sometime occupied by Richard Burles and late of William Burrill'. Hawkes Bros., Confectioners, began their business in Duke's Head Yard adjoining the bridge. It would be interesting to know whether Richard Burles was a forebear of the late Mr. A.J. Burls, one of the partners of Hawkes Bros. at that time.

THE OLD BOROUGH COAT OF ARMS

The two crossed crosiers on the shield are emblematic of the connections of the See of London and the Abbey of Westminster with Chelmsford and Moulsham, which comprised the Borough at the time of its incorporation.

The bridge of three arches in the centre of the shield represents the historic bridge built over the River Can by Maurice, Bishop of London and Lord of the Manor of Chelmsford about the year 1100.

The lions rampant above the bridge have been introduced into the Arms as a record of the Mildmay family, whose shield bore three lions rampant; and the two "bars wavy" at the base of the shield symbolise the ford of the River Chelmer, from which Chelmsford takes its name.

In the Crest which surmounts the Arms, the two crossed swords represent the arms of the See of London; the crosier represents the Abbey of Westminster; and the circlet of oak leaves is emblematic of English municipal freedom.

CHAPTER IV

WITCHCRAFT – THE TRIALS OF WITCHES
AT CHELMSFORD

THERE ALWAYS HAS been, and no doubt there always will be, a feeling of superstition in the minds of many people, about witchcraft and ghosts. In the 17th century there appears to have been a wide belief in witchcraft. Men of learning and men of science gave credance and fatal support to the masses in this evil craft. It was, however, treated as a hideous crime, punishable by death. Many thousands were burnt at the stake during the Commonwealth – the Puritans were particularly zealous in putting into force the laws against it.

Essex had a witchfinder of great repute – Mathew Hopkins, of Manningtree, and he cast his net widely. Court was held at Chelmsford to try the victims he had caught. Convictions and burnings for witchcraft had not been uncommon, and it was thought of as naturally as that of murder or horse stealing. But on one occasion in the year 1645 Hopkins had rounded up a number of so-called witches, all of them old women, raked up from the villages of the county. Twenty-five were dragged to the Shirehouse at Chelmsford and indicted for holding direct communion with the devil, entertaining and nourishing imps, and by their instrumentality working mischief upon the cattle and persons of their neighbours.

These helpless and infirm old women hobbled into the dock, mumbling words of fear through their toothless gums and withered lips, called upon to answer with their lives for every threatening word, and committed to the flames on the faith of village gossip.

The evidence was generally of the most frivolous character, 'and such as would not now be held sufficient to justify the infliction of a 5s. fine upon a poacher'. To have an enemy who had died suddenly, or a neighbour afflicted with some strange disorder, especially if a small wen or wart (which were the teats the imps were supposed to suck) was found on the body of the accused, were taken as conclusive proofs of guilt.

These witches appear to have been very commonplace creatures. There was nothing romantic about their mischief. They mixed no deadly pottage; they bid no 'hell-broth boil and bubble' in the dark cave, or beneath the gibbet, or on the wild heath, with mysterious incantations – they saddled and bridled no broomsticks for equestrian excursions amongst the clouds. They were all charged with being actuated by feelings of paltry spite.

The most extraordinary aspect, however, was that some of the victims confessed all that was charged against them, which can only be explained by the supposition that they were imbecile or insane, or terrified and bewildered by the pompous array of justice, or weak or ignorant in mind. In some cases the confessions were extracted by torture. The accused were worn out and wearied by watchers, who prevented them from sleeping for three or four nights on end. They were walked about until their feet blistered. Others were subjected to the test of swimming, according to the rule laid down by King James in his book on demonology, that 'witches deny their baptism when they covenant with the devil, and water being the sole element thereof, therefore when they be heaved into the water, the water refuseth to receive them into its bosom, and suffers them to float'.

The justices on the bench must have been naive and highly superstitious, believing the nonsense offered as evidence. 'Learned clergymen appeared in the witness box, detailing such examples as the employment of imps employed by the witches, and sending them to assail a child or a neighbour' the reverend gentleman adding 'to his own knowledge' about the child being taken strangely ill and in a short time dying'.

Secondhand evidence or hearsay was accepted as evidence, such as one justice who assumed the role of judge and witness and violated all the then accepted rules of evidence by relating from the bench, at second hand, a goblin story which he had heard to the effect that passing the door of a reputed witch one morning he looked inquisitively in at the door, and was forth-with assailed by four black rabbits, and finding he could not kill them by blows of his stick, he seized one, took the body of it in one hand and the head of it in the other, and as he wrung and stretched the neck of it, it came out between his hands like a lock of wool. Drown the imps, he could not, though he held them at arm's length in a stream, and at length they vanished into the air.

Very few of the accused escaped; 10 were executed at Chelmsford; one died on the way to execution, and two in gaol. Four were burnt at the stake. In 1579 three witches from Maldon were also tried and executed at Chelmsford in front of the Shire Hall.

CHAPTER V

THE GAOLS OF CHELMSFORD

THE STONE BRIDGE which was known as the Bishop's Bridge because it was built by Bishop Maurice, is shown on the print on page   ; the print was taken from an old painting and was made in 1810.

You will see on the south-western end of the Bridge, where Fosters, the Clothiers, now stands, the Old County Gaol; this was the first gaol in Chelmsford, although there was formerly a House of Correction which stood in the centre of High Street opposite Springfield Road on the site occupied by Baxters', the Butchers.

It is interesting to note the soldiers in the print. Early in the 19th century troops were continuously passing through the town. Officers' barracks were then in Coval Lane, while the men were quartered in Barrack Square, opposite Baddow Road; the site is now occupied by Debenhams Furniture Store on the one side and the Co-operative Society on the other.

The first pile of the old prison was driven on 3rd September 1773, and the building was first occupied on 19th October 1777.

About 50 years after the prison had been erected it was resolved to abandon 'the inconvenient building and the unhealthy site', and the new Gaol in Springfield Road, abutting upon Sandford Road, was built. The first brick was laid by Sir John Tyrrell on 22nd October 1822, and the building was completed in 1828, at a cost of £57,289.17s.0¾d., enlarged in 1849 and improved in 1871.

The old Gaol by the Stone Bridge was subsequently occupied as a Militia Depot and continued as such until almost the turn of the century.

The last Governor of the Old Gaol was one Thomas Clarkson Neale, who was appointed Governor of the new prison in Springfield Road. Mr. Neale was a geologist and antiquarian, and founded the Chelmsford Philosophical Society from which sprang the Museum. The first exhibition of Museum objects was held in Mr. Neale's parlour. When he died his collection of fossils was presented to the Museum by his daughter.

D.W. Coller records that from his prison cell at the Old Gaol one Rev. G.S. Clarke watched the arrival and departure of the coaches at the Old Ship Inn which was, of course, a short distance along High Street (on the opposite side to the Gaol) going towards Springfield Road, approximately on the site now occupied by Trueform Shoes.

The Rev. Clarke was imprisoned for not conforming to the then authorised version of the Bible.

The corner site on the northern corner of Springfield Road, at present occupied by Discount Carpet Warehouse, must house some ghosts, if ghosts there be. And if you will look at the print on page 29 you will see shown there Springfield Road corner and the building which was occupied by Chelmsford Post Office and The Old Black Boy; this was in the year 1762. But before that, in the 15th and 16th centuries, The Crown Inn stood on the site, this inn was also sometimes called The King's Arms, because a room was set aside and known as 'The Sheriff's Prison' in which were placed the King's Arms.

It was to the Sheriff's Prison that George Eagles, alias Trudgeon, was taken after being apprehended on the main road near Colchester for treason. He stood trial at the Old Sessions House at Chelmsford and was charged and afterwards conveyed to the Crown. Eagles' sentence is supposed to have been carried out at Rainsford End, the local Tyburn.

There was in 1807 still a field on the spot, on the old Tithe Map, marked 'Gallows Field', and it was from this fact that the lane which adjoined Gallows Field leading from the high road at Rainsford End to Waterhouse Lane was called Gallows Lane.

Hundreds of criminals have suffered for various offences at Gallows Field.

The case of George Eagles is recounted by D.W. Coller. He was a tailor, with little or no learning, but 'being eloquent and of good utterance', he set up as a preacher and, travelling from place to place, and from county to county, to exhort and encourage the suffering Protestants, he obtained the nickname of 'Trudgeover'. He was compelled to hide in the fields and woods, a royal proclamation having been sent through Essex and three other counties, offering a reward of £20 for his apprehension.

One day he was recognised in Colchester, and fled. The mob, with their zeal quickened by the promised gold, hunted him into the country. He was caught in a corn field, and taken to London, but was afterwards sent to Chelmsford for trial. The charge against him was high treason for having seditiously assembled companies of more than six together; he was also further accused of having on one occasion prayed that 'God

40

would turn Queen Mary's heart, or take her away'.

He was doomed to a traitor's death. He was carried to the new inn, called The Sign of the Crown, in Chelmsford, by the bailiffs. Later he was laid on a sled, with a hurdle on it, and drawn to the place of execution, (the Market Cross outside the Shire Hall), being fast bound, having in his hand a psalm book, from which he read very devoutly all the way with a loud voice till he reached the place of execution.

Shortly after he had been hanged, one of the bailiffs cut the halter, and he fell to the ground, but was still alive. One of the bailiffs, William Swallow, of Chelmsford, then pulled him on to the sled on which he had been brought to the gallows, and laid his neck on it, and with 'a cleaver such as is occupied in many men's kitchens, and blunt, did hackle off his head; and sometimes hit his neck, and sometimes hit his chin, and did foully mangle him, and so opened him'.

Then William Swallow 'did pluck out his heart'.

The body was then divided into four parts, and his bowels burnt; one part of the body remained at Chelmsford, one was carried to Colchester, another to Harwich and the other to St. Rouse's. His head was set up at Chelmsford on the Market Cross, on a long pole, till the wind blew it down, where it lay for some days, until someone had it buried in the churchyard during the night.

He was not the only victim of the times; many others suffered a similar fate. Thomas Watts, a linen-draper of Billericay, had been condemned in London, and carried to an inn in Chelmsford, and after taking leave of his wife and six children, was burnt at the stake in Chelmsford.

A report in *The Times*, of 26th March 1851, headed 'The Chelmsford Executions', records (1) that on the previous morning Thomas Drory and Sarah Chesham, the perpetrators of two horrible and barbarous murders expiated their crimes by an ignominious death in front of the County Gaol at Springfield. Drory had strangled a girl, the daughter-in-law of an old servant of his father, whom he had seduced, and was the father of the child she was expecting. She had met him to ask him to marry her; he then produced a piece of rope and strangled her and left her in a field and went off to Brentwood.

(2) Sarah Chesham was a poisoner, having poisoned her child. She was 42 years of age, and had the reputation of a poisoner but had always managed to get off previous charges. She poisoned her husband by small doses of arsenic.

The report ends: 'In little more than an hour after the bodies were cut down, that of Drory was buried within the precincts of the Gaol.' All applications for a cast of his head were rigidly refused. It was decided that this could not be turned to any useful purpose and would only feed the morbid curiosity of coarse and ignorant minds.

The body of Sarah Chesham was not buried within the precincts of the Gaol, having been claimed by a relative.

De Vere Coat of Arms: Quarterly gules and or in the first quarter a mullet argent. Crest the sun shining on a sun flower proper.

THE DE VERE FAMILY

THE PRINT of The Black Boy Inn on page 49 is later than the 1762 print; all the buildings shown in Springfield Road are now empty to make room for the development of the area and the widening of the road.

Dickens mentions The Black Boy in *Pickwick Papers*, when Mr. Weller, senior, relates how he transported Job Trotter and Charles Fitz-Marshall from 'The Black Boy at Chelmsford..... right through to Ipswich'. Dickens himself, after attending court hearings in Norwich, often stopped off at The Black Boy on his way back to London to report the cases, staying the night at the inn.

It is thought that the house once belonged to the De Vere Family, formerly of Hedingham Castle. The Blue Boar was one of the principal badges of this family, and in the Chelmsford Museum can be seen a wooden boss taken from the ceiling of a room of The Old Black Boy when it was pulled down in 1857, having been run off the road by the opening of the railway in 1843.

John De Vere, who succeeded to the title in 1415, is presumed to have been in constant communication with the court and undoubtedly would have journeyed to and from Hedingham Castle, his baronial seat, to London many times in the course of the year; as it would appear that the old hostelry, The Black Boy, belonged to the De Veres, it is fair to assume that the Earl and his retainers upon the occasions of their journey to London, stayed at this inn As the Earl lived in almost royal state, his comings to and fro would have been a matter of as much importance to the townsfolk as a visit of the sovereign. His shield, charged with the mullet, carved in the spandrel of the west door of the tower of Chelmsford Cathedral, is an indication that he may have assisted to a large extent in the cost of the building of the Cathedral (then the parish church) in 1424.

For five centuries did this mighty family rule most royally over many parts of the country, their riches being immense, and their power and influence being second only to the sovereign. Alas, they were reduced to the lowest ebb of poverty and distress after the Wars of the Roses; and now a cubic foot of stone in our Cathedral and a cubic foot of oak deposited in our Museum are all that remain in this town to remind us of them.

CHAPTER VII

JUDGE TINDAL

THE STATUE of Lord Chief Justice Tindal was erected by subscription of the inhabitants of Chelmsford to their great legal townsman. Originally, it occupied the site of the old Conduit, the origin of which is of unknown date. There is no doubt, however, that at a very early date the pure water flowing from the spring of Burgess' Well (which is in the garden of No. 15 Fairfield Road) was greatly appreciated by the inhabitants, and that some building of the kind stood on the spot for the purpose of receiving the stream, and distributing it through the various streets.

In 1750 it was an erection of brick (see the print on page 91), and it then bore the following inscription: 'This conduit, in one minute, runs 1 hogshead and ½ and 4 gallons and ½. In one day 2,262 hogsheads and 54 gallons. In one month 63,360 hogsheads. And in one year 825,942 hogsheads and 54 gallons.' (They seem to have had 13-month years in those days. I make 12 times 63,360, 760,320 hogsheads.)

The parishioners were very proud of this water supply; it was a feature in the town mentioned by every historian; and the noble families of Fitzwalters and Mildmays liberally endeavoured to improve and perpetuate it. Sir William Mildmay, in 1771, bequeathed £200 in trust for the purpose. The former building was surmounted by the royal arms, with those of the Duke of Schomberg and Earl Fitzwalter.

The stone conduit was erected in 1814 by means of subscription, added to a legacy of £100 from a Mr. Robert Greenwood, and subsequently a Mr. Thomas Chalk gave the rent of a house to secure the proper care and guardianship of the well. Later, possibly in consequence of the Board of Trade's having adopted an artesian well for the water supply of the town, the advantages of the spring from Burgess Well appear to have been discarded. The conduit was moved in 1852 to High Street opposite Springfield Road (see the photograph on page 69) and remained there until 1940 when it was placed in Tower Gardens, Rainsford End.

During the recent development of the area of Tindal Square and Tindal Street, the statue of Judge Tindal has been moved away from the original spot to a point nearer Tindal Street.

Judge Tindal was born at Coval Hall and was educated at Chelmsford Grammar School.

The photograph of the Conduit at Springfield Road corner on page 69 was taken probably in the early 1900s. It is an interesting one, and shows part of the railings of Barnards Temperance Hotel which were removed when the building was demolished and the development of the corner took place and the street widened.

STATUE OF SIR NIC* TINDAL
CHELMSFORD

45

CHAPTER VIII

THE GHOST OF WATERLOO CHAMBERS

WATERLOO CHAMBERS was until recent years occupied by Luckin & Sheldrake, the Accountants; prior to that the site was occupied variously as a boarding house and a tavern. But in the year 1654 it was occupied as the Inn known as 'The White Horse Inn', which was the scene of a horrible murder, the perpetrators of which were not brought to justice until 13 years later; before the trial, in fact, took place, two of the murderers had died.

The full report of the case entitled *A True Relation of a Horrid Murder committed upon the Person of Thomas Kidderminster at the White Horse Inn in Chelmsford in the County of Essex, in the month of April 1654* consists of 20 quarto-sized sheets of gruesome details which I finally ran to earth after some months of searching.

Thomas Kidderminster, the murdered man, was a farmer from Ely, who was on his way to London to rejoin his wife who had previously left Ely to visit relations while her husband completed the sale of his farm and wound up the remainder of his affairs at Ely. His wife had expected him to rejoin her in about 10 days.

Instead of travelling the direct route to London, he went with a guide via Chelmsford as he was carrying a large sum of money in gold, and deeds and papers relating to his properties, including those of his estate at Tupsley in the County of Hereford, which had been wrongfully taken from him by his stepmother and stepfather after his parents died when he was 11 years of age. It was primarily to endeavour to regain his property at Tupsley that he retired from farming and was on his way to London.

He paid off his guide when he reached Chelmsford and put up at the White Horse Inn, which he had done on a number of occasions before. He had known the host, Mr. Sewell, and his wife and daughters, for a number of years.

From the time he entered the inn on that evening in April 1654 he was never seen again; his remains were discovered years later buried in the yard.

When Mrs. Kidderminster left Ely for London she was pregnant; a daughter was born in the following August.

Because of her condition she was unable to search for her

husband, but she was assisted in her enquiries by the parson who married them and who had called upon her in London to see Thomas Kidderminster on a matter of business; the enquiries came to nought.

Mrs. Kidderminster, in the year 1663, was living with her sister in London, when she read in the daily newspaper a report of the discovery of the bones of an unknown person, supposed to have been murdered, in the backyard of premises in Chelmsford. Upon comparing the time of her husband's disappearance with the time mentioned in the newspaper of the supposed murder, her suspicious were again aroused, and she set to work once more in an endeavour to find the cause of her husband's disappearance.

The result of her enquiries eventually revealed that when Thomas Kidderminster arrived at the inn he told Sewell and his wife that the cloak-bag which he handed to him for safe custody for the night contained £600 in gold and writings of considerable value; this was said in the presence of a serving maid who gave evidence at the trial and who stated that between one and two in the morning she had heard the sound of something heavy falling in one of the rooms of the house. This was corroborated by two women, one a washer-woman passing the White Horse Inn between one and two in the morning when she heard a voice crying out: 'What! Will you rob me of my money and murder me too? If you take my money, spare my life.' Then she heard something that fell very heavily. The lights were then put out, and no further noise heard.

Another witness said that Sewell had killed Kidderminster by hitting him on the side of the head with a pole axe, and Mrs. Sewell, with the help of her daughter, Betty, had slit his throat and 'blooded him into the Hogs-pail'.

The body was buried by Sewell with the help of his ostler, Moses Drayne, who received £60 and Kidderminster's suit and hat.

The burial place was discovered by chance when Mr. Turner, the then host of the White Horse Inn, had occasion to erect a wall between his garden and that of his neighbour in place of a fence which would never remain standing despite all efforts. The building of the wall entailed the digging of a ditch; and it was then that the skull of Kidderminster was unearthed and the remainder of the corpse discovered, which appeared to have been 'cramm'd in double'. There was a hole on the left side of the skull.

Turner took the skull and threw it over into the orchard 'where the grass was high and ready to mow'. The skull was observed to run *uphill*, and through the thick grass, for a dozen yards, towards the house, till it stopped against a fallen tree. He followed it, thinking there might be something alive in it that caused it so to move, but when he found it there was nothing in it but dirt and gravel.

The report continues with details of Mrs. Kidderminster's enquiries, and records that she stayed at the White Horse one night and slept in a room adjoining that in which her husband had been murdered. She was awakened by noises in the adjoining room 'which went out into the Gallery, where something seem'd to fall with that violence, that she thought the room shook, and afterwards came to her Chamber-door, and lifted the Latch'. Mrs. Kidderminster awakened the serving maid sleeping in the same room, and the noise immediately ceased. Mrs. Kidderminster told Mr. Turner, the host, of this, who said that these things had been heard many times before, and was thought to be the ghost of Thomas Kidderminster.

I have never heard that Waterloo Chambers is haunted — except, perhaps, by the staggering figures produced by the accountants over the years!

Sewell became ill and died a fortnight before he was due to appear at the Assizes; it was suspected that he was poisoned by his wife because he was showing signs of going mad since the bones had been found and she was afraid he would implicate her and her daughter.

The woman who had done the inn's washing on the day following the murder had been examined before a Justice of the Peace, and under oath denied that any blood had been found on the linen, adding 'that if there was any such she wish'd she might rot alive'. Shortly afterwards 'her Bowels began to rot away, and she became detestably loathsome till she died'.

Mrs. Sewell died of the Plague before the final trial.

Moses Drayne, the ostler, was found guilty and was hanged.

The serving maid was sent to prison for life for perjury.

The two daughters of Sewell were discharged and found not guilty for lack of evidence.

At the time of the report Mrs. Kidderminster was still endeavouring to obtain possession of her husband's estate at Tupsley; this was proving to be extremely difficult as all the

48

The Black Boy Inn c.1850.

Nickols & Jeffreys, High Street, c.1905.

49

The High Street, looking

...n the Shire Hall, c.1900

Duke Street in the late 1800's

Broomfield Road Corner

52

deeds and papers relating to the property had been lost when Thomas Kidderminster was murdered.

Next to the White Horse Inn was another inn known as The Star, probably on the site of the old Post Office.

Adjoining the old Post Office was the Saracen's Head; it is mentioned in the 1591 Survey by reference — one Rycharde Brett held 'one parcell of waste land north to south XV feet by VI feet east to west, to have moveable stalls to be used in market time lying before the Saracens Head'.

The Saracen's Head was, however, in existence even earlier and Sir Walter Scott refers to it in a 15th century setting. A much later association is with the name of Anthony Trollope who often stayed there; when he was Inspector General of the Post Office he visited it frequently both on business and for hunting.

Chelmsford just before the fire of 1808

CHAPTER IX

THE CHURCH

THE CATHEDRAL CHURCH of Saint Mary the Virgin, Saint Peter and Saint Cedd is the parish church of Chelmsford.

The building is relatively small for a cathedral. The size is not important: in fact, what is important, is that the Bishop of Chelmsford has his seat, or cathedra, here.

The date of origin of the church is not known; it is of very ancient date, so ancient that the date of its erection and the name of its founder are hidden in the mists of the past. There is little doubt that a church existed in Chelmsford in Saxon times, perhaps in connection with a monastery, and long before the Bishops of London obtained possession of it.

The character of the church was somewhat changed in 1424 when it was partly rebuilt, repaired and restored.

Fragments of Norman work have been found in the walling of the tower, and it is recorded that up to the end of the 18th century an inscription in letters a foot long, formed of flint, appeared 'beneath the battlements fronting the town', giving the date 1424.

In 1642 Chelmsford was the rendezvous of all the men enlisted for the parliamentary army; and in November of that year the church suffered from great violence of a mob of Puritans and Brownists and Anabaptists who not only destroyed the east window, described as the window 'through which the sun threw its dim religious light' upon the worshippers, but the town was a scene of other acts of riotous violence. The *Book of Common Prayer* was taken from the church and torn to pieces, and its tattered leaves scattered about in triumph. Bonfires were kindled in all the streets, and the rector, who had been fired at through a window, was obliged to fly for his life.

The church suffered a further tragedy in 1800. At about 10 o'clock on the night of 12th January of that year, the greater part of the walls, with the whole of the roof, fell with a crash which roused the inhabitants from their supper tables or their slumbers, and, rushing to the churchyard, they beheld the fine old stone tower standing erect and firm, but the great body of the church was gone, and pulpit and pews, altar and tomb, lay buried beneath a mass of shapeless ruins. The immediate cause of the disaster was attributed to the loosening and under-mining of a part of the wall in the course of preparing a vault between the pillars, near the porch; but centuries of time must have sapped the sacred pile, or the whole would not have been brought down by a relatively minor excavation.

The church was rebuilt in three years and was re-opened on 18th September 1803; in the meantime, divine service was held in the Shire Hall.

Extensions and alterations have been made to the Cathedral during the past century, including the erection of the galleries in the north and south aisles and at the west end. That at the west end was removed in 1867; the others in 1873 when the outer north aisle was added, together with the north transept to house the organ chamber and vestries. In 1899 the present timber roofs replaced older ones. The height of the Cathedral from the ground to the top of the battlements of the tower is about 90 feet.

Full details of all extensions and replacements and much more besides can be seen in Geoffrey Wrayford's Guide.

St. John's Church, in Upper Moulsham, built in the early English style, was erected as a Chapel of Ease in 1841, on land given by Lady Mildmay, at a cost of £2500. It has since been considerably enlarged in recent years.

In addition to the Cathedral and St. John's Church there were three Independent Chapels, one on the site adjoining the Bridge in London Road now occupied by the Co-operative Society; this was the Congregational Chapel which was built in 1840 at a cost of £5000. It was capable of holding 2000 people. Another of the Independent Chapels was the Old Meeting House in Baddow Road — probably one of the oldest in the county, tradition carrying it back for at least four centuries; the third chapel was 'amidst the clustering population of the Town Field'. The Town Field is now occupied by Rectory Road and Marconi Road and Marconi's Works. The chapel was opposite the Cemetery in Rectory Road. As I have already mentioned the Bishop's House was also on part of this area and was demolished when Marconi's Works was built.

Also on the site of Marconi's Works were two wireless masts reaching 450 feet into the sky. These were dismantled in 1935. In the 1920's one of the masts was damaged in a heavy thunderstorm, and part of the structure at the top broke loose and fell to the ground. Old Chelmsfordians will remember the steeple jack, Mr. Fred Post, climbing, unaided except for a bosun's sling around his waist, to the top of the mast (450 feet high) to repair the damage and enable the mast to be used again.

The other churches remaining in the town are the Roman Catholic Church in New London Road, erected in 1846, at an outlay of £2500, The Baptist Chapel adjoining the Hospital in New London Road, built in 1842, and The Wesleyan Chapel now united with Trinity Methodist Church, Rainsford End, which was primarily in Springfield Road adjoining Horsepond Bridge and, later, on the site of Caters Stores.

The site on which Caters Stores is built has an interesting background. Around the end of the 15th centurey, circa 1497, the site was occupied by the Cocke Inn; it was a famous old hostelrie described as 'situate on the east side of High Street and abutting on the Old Stone Bridge'.

It covered a frontage of 57 feet and a depth of 125 feet to a backwater known as The Gullet, and the garden which was approached by a small bridge over the latter measuring 62 feet by 92 feet, and a vehicular entrance by the side of the Stone Bridge.

The Old Cocke Inn, however, was in existence during the Plague of 1603—4, and also during the Plague of 1665. During the latter period of the Plague, such was the demand for graves that in some instances people were actually buried in the gardens or orchards attached to their houses. According to tradition this was the case of the Old Cocke Inn; whether any skeletons were found when digging the foundations for the Wesleyan Chapel is not recorded. The Wesleyan Chapel was erected on the site in 1847 at a cost of £7000. It was built of red brick and stone with an octagonal tower, and afforded sittings for 650 persons; attached were commodious class and school rooms for 500 children. It was demolished in 1971, and Caters Stores took its place.

The Old Stone Bridge was replaced by the present bridge in 1788; work was commenced on the new bridge in 1785 and re-opened on 14th January 1788. The traffic in the meantime was routed 'via Baddow Lane, crossing the river by a wooden bridge, and entering Springfield Lane at the rear of The King's Head'.

The Friends' Meeting House was in Duke Street, opposite the Railway Station. The Quakers used it and held meetings there from 1824 to 1957. The building is now occupied by the Mid-Essex Technical College and School of Art.

St. Peter's Church was erected in 1802; in addition to its being a place of worship, it has a history of great musical achievement, mainly due to the hard work and devotion of William (Billy) Bush, its choirmaster and conductor over a period of 60 years. He celebrated his diamond jubilee as organist of the church in 1960. Billy Bush's tutor, Frederick Frye, also attained his diamond jubilee as organist of Chelmsford Cathedral some years earlier.

Other denominations have since the end of the 19th century built places of worship in the town amongst which are the Primitive Methodist in Hall Street and the United Reformed Church, Christchurch, in New London Road.

JOSEPH STRUTT,

AGED ABOUT 50.

From a pencil sketch by himself.

In 1907 the Grammar School was divided into 'houses' after the names of famous old Chelmsfordians, one of whom was Joseph Strutt; the others were Sir Walter Mildmay, Sir Nicholas Tindal and Dr. Philemon Holland.

CHAPTER X

THE NAPOLEONIC WARS

AT THE OUTBREAK of hostilities with France in 1802 Moulsham was the scene of great activity.

Chelmsford raised £10,000 for building up the defences of the country; camps were set up in many places in the county including one at Galleywood (this may be the origin of the name 'Watchhouse Lane', Galleywood), of entrenchment from the Common to Widford, and a battery set up in Long Stomps.

Many of the inhabitants enrolled themselves in an infantry corps of volunteers, under the command of Major Gepp; and a set of colours was presented to them with all the pomp and parade of a public ceremonial, by the Misses Morgan, from a platform in front of Mr. Coates' house in Baddow Road. This corps, when united with the Baddow volunteers under Captain Hull, and the Writtle contingent under Captain Barlow, formed a very efficient regiment. Others joined a cavalry troop under Captain Tufnell, which continued embodied until 1828.

The town swarmed with troops of the line. The barracks at both ends of the town were full and temporary buildings were raised for 3000 others. With the camps at Galleywood, the number of troops in the neighbourhood amounted to 8 — 10 thousand.

It was at this time (1804) that a sad catastrophe in connection with this crowded state of the town occurred. On 22nd October, a body of Hanoverian troops arrived and, as accommodation could not be found for all, 70 of them, with several women, fatigued with their long march, lay down to sleep in a stable at the Spotted Dog in Back Street. The pipes of the inveterate German smokers speedily ignited the straw. On the first occasion the fire was extinguished; but about eight o'clock the whole building was found to be in flames. The door was only latched but, ignorant of the mode of opening it, they had no means of escape till succour came from without. Then a crowd of burning men rushed wildly about the yard and street.

It was thought all had escaped; but one died of his injuries, and 12 charred corpses were taken from the ruins. The whole garrison turned out at the funeral on the following Friday and lined the streets with their arms reversed as 13 coffins passed up to one grave in the churchyard, over which a huge mound was raised, and long marked the resting place of the friendly foreigners who thus perished. A monument was later erected in the churchyard, near the Shire Hall.

One of the barracks was built on the site of the present St. John's Hospital in Wood Street. Prior to its being used as a hospital it was the Workhouse, but in the Estate and Family Archives D/UU 116-143 at the Records Office at Chelmsford is a record of 'land purchased by "Wm.W" on behalf of the Crown for the erection of barracks for the Army'. It is described as a close of land (7a) called 'Oxneys' in the occupation of Thomas Coombs in Moulsham in Chelmsford. This land has been identified as that on which the hospital stands. The barracks, however, were pulled down in 1828 and the Workhouse erected thereon.

* * * * * * * *

Four years after the fire in which the Hanoverian soldiers were burnt to death at the Spotted Dog, the Great Fire of Chelmsford occurred. A Narrative by an eye-witness can be seen at the Records Office. It is described as 'The Late Deplorable Fire at Chelmsford' and occurred on Saturday morning, 19th March 1808.

The author heads the narrative with: 'O!, I have suffered with those that I saw. Care did knock at my heart; poor souls, they perish'd. Shakespeare Tampest. (sic).'

The fire ravaged a considerable part of the town and left several families entirely destitute and houseless, besides the vast destruction of property, and striking inexpressible terror into the neighbourhood in general.

The fire was first observed about 3 a.m. in the dining room of Mrs. Smith, Milliner; if you look at the sketch drawn by the author and shown on page 70 you will see her house and shop were approximately where New London Road and High Street now meet, on the site of Walkers, the Jewellers. It was then described as the front house in the Middle Row — which was the name of the whole line of shops from London Road corner to the Shire Hall. Flames at the time issued from the windows, and particularly furiously at one adjoining the dwelling of 'Mrs. Peck, the chemist, wakened by her servant who slept near her mistress in the same room. At this time burning flakes were falling on to the bed clothes. She was the first person who discovered the fire. Because when the family escaped into the street, not a living soul was to be seen besides themselves. The whole town appeared as if locked in a profound slumber.

'When the servant reached the front door of the shop the key was missing (this had been left in the bedroom). Mrs. Peck flew upstairs again and seized the key. At the same time, remembering her assistant in bed in the room above, and with a most happy presence of mind and extraordinary resolution rushed to his staircase (then enveloped in flames) and roused him from his sleep.

'When they reached the street, veiled by a heavy fall of snow . . . . they ran from door to door, ringing, knocking and calling for assistance and making most violent efforts to rouse their neighbours.

'Where was the watchman? He was nowhere to be seen or heard: had the watchmen been on their duty the dreadful catastrophe might have been either prevented or at least mitigated and valuable lives spared.

'Victims crashed through the floors of some houses and were burnt to death before help could reach them.' (Miss Wolmer was one).

One brave man attempted to rescue Miss Smith; 'he got her on to a ladder outside the window of her bedroom; she was naked and made it difficult to hold her. She convulsed with terror; he was unable to hold her and she fell from a great height with violence to the street.'

The rest of the inhabitants were roused, 'engines' (fire, I assume) 'were stationed, and the Chelmsford volunteers had assembled, and the officers and privates of the Garrison had arrived, and all classes, without distinction, were active in preserving the surrounding property. Mrs. Smith's and Mrs. Peck's houses were one great sheet of flame.'

The author adds: 'From the lower end of the town, (the fire) formed a magnificent and beautiful appearance of an immense illuminated cylindrical lamp producing an effect so sublime, awful and affecting as to impoverish all description.

'The extension of the fire was checked by the efforts of the Chelmsford volunteers operating the Phoenix Fire Engine, and succeeded in stopping the progress of the fire beyond houses in Back Street and the old timber buildings with the printing office, the theatre and a vast range of small dwellings, coach houses, stables and brew house.

'In about two hours the fire was to a degree arrested.

'The fire having received a material check, many houses

were preserved as it gave time for the extraordinary efforts of about 100 men, who regulated, supplying each other with empty and full buckets of water from the river.' (They were strung out along the yard of Kelham, the agent of the Phoenix Fire Office.) The water was used to dampen the fronts of the shops and the neighbouring houses.

Many people were burnt to death or killed jumping from upper windows.

'Some of the dwellings in the Back Street, near adjoining, occupied by Mr. Murrell, Corn Chandler, Mr. Sheppee, Currier, and Mr. Weedon, broker, were in such danger as to make a removal of their families and effects absolutely necessary. In attempting which, this last unfortunate man, who had long laboured under a severe and dangerous indisposition, by endeavouring to escape down stairs with a sick child, fell on his back and received so serious an injury that he has lain ever since without hope of recovery. The poor infant died a few days later.

'On the Tuesday morning a coroner's inquest assembled. In viewing the mutilated remains of the two young ladies which had been dug from the ruins, the office of coroner, being filled by an unmarried gentleman not far advanced in years, it was delicately and prudently suggested that Thos. Gepp Esq. should preside.

'The funeral was watched by the multitude; it was preceded by two men clearing the way, the sexton, clergymen, the undertaker and his assistants, 24 families, arm in arm, habited in white, the Parish Clerk, and many others; and at the end the chief mourners; the whole occupying a considerable part of the principal street through which they passed.'

Amongst the ruins of Mr. Hills' house a cat and several kittens (unharmed) were found.

CHAPTER XI

AFTER THE MILDMAY ENTAIL

EXTENSIVE development took place in Chelmsford
after the Mildmay entail had been broken.

On page 303 of the *Directory of Essex* (1848) by William
White is a description of the town at this time:

'The Town has been greatly improved during the last ten
years; the Conduit Square and High Street (where the market is
held) as well as the other principal streets, are well paved'
(P. Muilman, in his *History of Essex*, 1770, records that the
road surfaces were gravelled, sloping to the centre, and washed
by clear water running through) 'and lighted with gas. The
houses are generally modern, and many of them have gardens
behind them, extending to the river. There are in the Town
many large Inns and Taverns, and well-stocked shops, and some
of the latter have handsome plate glass windows.

'The Eastern Counties Railway was opened in 1843, and
crosses the western part of the Town and suburbs, by a Viaduct
of 18 brick arches, each 30 feet in span and 45 feet in height to
the top of the parapet. The Station is conveniently placed
between the two lines of rails, and approached by a double
staircase from the arch which crosses Duke Street.

'In 1839 the Town was closely encompassed by entailed
land, belonging to the Mildmay family, but in that year the
estate became disentailed; and about 400 acres of land adapted
for building was sold for about £80,000 in lots to suit
purchasers.

'A new road, about a mile long, now called New London
Road, was set out through the property in Moulsham hamlet;
and it has since been continued into the centre of the Town by
a company of shareholders, who created a handsome cast iron
bridge over the river Can, and formed New Bridge Street, at
the cost of more than £5000; the old Theatre and a number of
houses etc. having to be purchased and removed, and about
10,000 square yards of earth to be carted for the formation of
this grand entrance to the Town.

'In 1841, another Company erected in the New road, at
the cost of £2500, an elegant building in the Grecian style,
called The Institute.' (It is still standing and the figures '1841'
are shown in the stonework over the main entrance.) 'It has
since been sold to Messrs. J. & E. Copland, but will be partly

occupied by the Literary & Mechanics Institution. Since that period the lower part of the road has been lined with well-built shops and private houses, and in New Bridge Street an elegant row of houses, called Museum Terrace has been erected by Mr. G. Meggy in the Roman style with corinthian pilasters.

'New chapels for the Roman Catholics, Independents and Baptists, and several highly ornamental mansions have recently been erected in other parts of the road; and many of them are honourable testimonials of the architectural skill of Mr. Fenton.

'The Half Moon Public House will obstruct the entrance to the High Street, but it is hoped it will soon be removed.' (It was removed during the year 1900-1901.)

The town was well-placed for industrial development between London and the Continent; and no doubt this attracted Cromptons to the town in 1878, Christy Brothers in 1883, Hoffmanns in 1899 and Marconis in 1900.

All these events were contributory to the development of the town and increased the town's administrative importance; and in 1888 it was incorporated as a Borough. (See the print of the procession on page 92.) In 1889 the Essex County Council set up its offices in Duke Street and, in 1908, Chelmsford became the Cathedral town of a new diocese.

Population was now increasing by nearly 400 persons a year.

In 1901 it had reached 12,627; by 1921 there were 20,769 in the Borough and 24,545 in the Rural District. This growth steadily continued and, in October 1944, the population of the Borough was estimated at 33,500. It is now about 70,000.

Following the cutting of New London Road and New Bridge Street, other roads were built in the town.

The Corn Exchange (see the photograph on page 91), which was built in 1831 and opened on 5th June of that year, replacing the old one in front of the Shire Hall, was considered at that time a fine building; it was demolished in May 1969 during the development of the shopping precinct.

The New London Road was cut through the green pastures and arable lands of the Mildmay Estate, and very soon the area was transformed by the building of Cromptons, the Railway and the many grand houses along the new road.

The Hospital was built in 1883 and was opened by the Countess of Warwick on 15th November of that year.

Until recently the Congregational Church stood in New London Road, opposite the Institute, but was demolished during the recent development; and the site is occupied partly by a row of shops and partly by the entrance leading to Friars Walk.

The Rural District Council offices in New London Road were built in 1938; formerly this authority was housed in Waterloo Lane in offices erected in 1913 adjoining the old Post Office yard. The R.D.C. is now incorporated in the Chelmsford District Council and New Bridge Street long ago merged into New London Road.

The photograph on page 72, taken from the front of the Shire Hall, shows High Street in 1876; the street must have been a quagmire in the winter!

The line of buildings has changed only slightly since the date of the photograph; the old buildings were demolished and others erected in their stead.

The Saracen's Head on the left-hand side of the photograph was then kept by a Mr. Moull; and you can see his surname over the side door of the building. This hotel was then as it is now, one of the principal hotels in the town. The old Town Jury Club and Beafsteak Club were held at this hotel; and every evening you would see a number of regular businessmen of the town enjoying a drink and talking of the day's business. They always sat in what was regarded as their own seat and, if a stranger or a non-regular was found to be sitting in the chair of one of the regulars, he was told firmly but politely that the seat was reserved, and he would be moved before the 'regular' arrived.

Immediately adjoining the Saracens Head was Fred Spalding's shop; he was primarily a photographer but he also sold a variety of fancy goods and knick-knacks of quality.

Next to Spalding's was a double-fronted shop occupied by a Mr. and Mrs. Freeston. On one side of the shop were sold caps and bonnets, very fashionable in those days, and on the other side Mr. Freeston sold leather goods and gloves.

Poole, the Saddler, was next; and then Pertwee, the Chemist.

No. 5 High Street was occupied by Dr. Gilson; in later years there was a passage way between the southern side of Spalding's shop and Dr. Gilson's, known as Crane Court. It was a narrow passage, not more than 15 feet wide, which led to the County Court Offices.

No. 6 High Street was a Baby-linen shop.

Then came Westminster Bank; it is still occupied as a Bank

but is, of course, now known as National Westminster Bank, a very modern building. Its predecessor was much more picturesque and imposing than the present one.

Next to the Bank was Medlicott's, the Tallow Chandlers, well-known to all the farmers for his candles which he made at his back premises. The small shops on the right of the photograph have been replaced by Midland Bank. The next building, beyond the narrow passage, has remained unchanged. Until recent years it was occupied by Alfred Darby & Co., the Auctioneers, now taken over by Strutt & Parker, who occupy the corner site of Duke Street opposite the new Post Office.

Duffields, the Solicitors, occupy the adjoining building shown in the photograph; that building has not changed either.

The old Conduit is just discernible in the distance; if you cannot see it with the naked eye in the photograph you will be able to see it with the aid of a magnifying glass.

The metal posts along the pathway on the right hand side of the street are the posts through which rope was looped and the animals tethered on market days.

Beyond the Conduit you can see a number of tall buildings on the left hand side of the street, almost as far as the Stone Bridge. Quite likely, the last building is the Militia Barracks which were still in existence at that time. (The Militia were disbanded in 1816; their Colours hang in the outer north aisle of the Cathedral.) It is said that the town's Surveyor always 'mended the roads' just before the annual training of the Militia, so that the men going to and from the Barracks to Moulsham and to Durrants Fields (now the Goods Station and Hoffmanns) trod the gravel in and thus saved the cost of rolling.

Looking again from the Shire Hall along High Street towards Springfield Road corner — on the right hand side, the first building was then occupied by Straight, the Grocer; later W.F. Call & Sons, also Grocers, took over the shop, and were succeeded by Mortimers in the same line of business.

Windows at that time were mostly semi-circular in shops, supported by an iron post in the centre, and had very small panes of glass. Most shops in Chelmsford had similar windows.

Further down from the Grocer's shop to Crown Passage, were the iron posts to which I have referred; these posts were embedded in the pavement and had, at the top of each and midway down, holes about three inches in diameter through which ropes were pulled, the object being to keep the cattle from straying on to the pavement. Often shop keepers found

65

a straying heifer, some sheep or other animals in his shop.

Fred Spalding tells of an old man named Miller; known locally as 'Dilly Miller' who was employed on market days to put the rope through the holes in the posts, and how he would start at the top end and pull the rope through to the end at the point approximately where Crown Passage is. Dilly would then tie a knot in the rope, go back to the top and pull the rope taut. In the evening the process was reversed.

The local boys would watch the old man and, as soon as he was halfway back, they would come out of Crown Passage (where they were hiding) and tie a knot in the end, so that when the old man pulled he could not get the rope through; he had to undo the knot and start again. Boyish pranks! It caused the old man undue trouble, but was of little moment when one considers the juvenile delinquency nowadays.

* * * * * * * *

From the steps of the Shire Hall, if you were to look over to the right beyond Tindal Square, you would see the Corn Exchange. Before the Corn Exchange was built, the Corn Market was held in the vestibule and outside the Shire Hall. The auctioneers and other agents also did their business there.

Between the Corn Exchange and the Golden Lion (now Strutt & Parker's offices), there was a space of only about 12 feet. In 1806 the late Brittain Pash, who owned the Agricultural Implement business in Market Road, opposite Threadneedle Street, erected a warehouse on the land. When the Cattle Market was built the Golden Lion was demolished and the road (Market Road) was opened; that was in 1879.

The 'Golden Lion' which replaced the original of that name was much smaller than the original and was erected on the site now occupied by Strutt & Parker.

The photograph of Tindal Square on page 91 shows that the square was paved with kidney or cobble stones. It was the same in front of the various shops in the town; also in front of the Corn Exchange, the Bell Hotel and The White Hart. The photograph of the Chelmsford Suffragettes on page 91 was taken in front of the Corn Exchange. The word 'Inn' of the Bell Inn can be seen in the top left-hand corner of the photograph and the entrance to the Corn Exchange on the extreme right.

The larger part of the Market was held in Tindal Square.

Ropes and posts were put up in front of the shops, similar to those in the High Street, and the horses stood facing the shops.

The old auctioneers were Alfred Darby and Joseph Wakeley, and they stood on stools when selling cattle by auction. Alfred Darby's office was then in High Street next to Duffields', the Solicitors. Duffields' was then a one-man firm.

The Pleasure Fair

The fairs of Chelmsford took place twice a year. They were held in the High Street and extended along both sides as far as Westminter Bank, while Tindal Square was full of booths and caravans. There were shows of all kinds: Cheap Jacks, Strong Men, Fat Women, Peep Shows, Clowns, Jugglers, Shooting Galleries and the rest.

Often as many as four roundabouts were to be seen in the streets — three in Tindal Square and one in front of the Cannon.

The Cannon, which stood on a plinth in front of the Shire Hall, is shown in the photograph on page 50 . The Cannon, a 36-pounder Russian gun, was installed there in July 1858; it now stands in Oaklands Park, having been moved from the Shire Hall site in September 1937. On the side of the plinth is inscribed:

'Sevastopol 1855. This carriage was presented by Major S.J. Skinner to the Town of Chelmsford in 1858 to commemorate the Chelmsford Agricultural Society's Show.'

Mr. Ted Cant, the custodian of the Car Park of Debenham's in Springfield Road, is a very old Chelmsfordian and knows a great deal about the town. He told me of an incident concerning Fred Spalding's shop; I cannot find a reference to it in the newspapers at the Record Office, but perhaps I had not the correct date. It occurred during the winter of 1913. It appears that a young boy of 14, named Harry Semayne, whose father was the publican of the King William IV at the wharf in Navigation Road, was asked by the Sergeant Farrier at the Drill Hall to take his horse to the Saracen's Head Yard for shoeing. He told the boy not to ride it; the boy could not ride a horse, anyway. However, he decided to try to ride it — with disastrous consequences. He mounted the horse, but the animal bolted; it raced down Duke Street with the boy clinging on for dear life. When it reached the end of Duke Street it dashed through Tindal Square and into High

Street, but the boy had lost control of the horse. He endeavoured to guide the horse towards the Saracen's Head Yard but it dashed straight into the window of Fred Spalding's shop. The boy was taken to hospital but was discharged the same evening. Harry Semayne survived; and later became a taxi driver in Chelmsford.

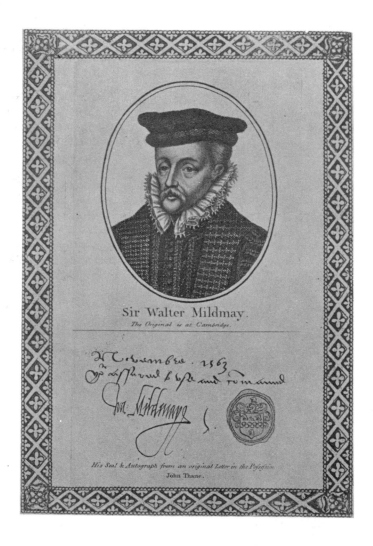

Sir Walter Mildmay.
The Original is at Cambridge.

His Seal & Autograph from an original Letter in the Possession
John Thane.

The Conduit, Springfield Road Corner

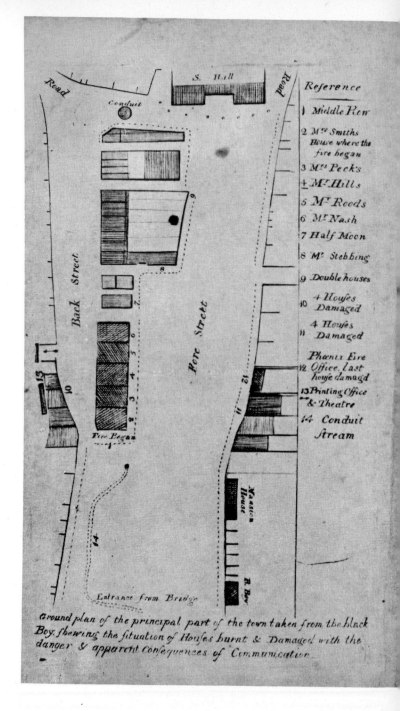

Reference

1 Middle Row
2 Mrs Smiths House where the fire began
3 Mrs Peck's
4 Mr Hills
5 Mr Roods
6 Mr Nash
7 Half Moon
8 Mr Stebbing
9 Double houses
10 4 Houses Damaged
11 4 Houses Damaged
12 Phœnix Fire Office, last house damag'd
13 Printing Office & Theatre
14 Conduit Stream

Ground plan of the principal part of the town taken from the Black Boy, shewing the situation of Houses burnt & Damaged with the danger & apparent Consequences of Communication

NARRATIVE

OF THE LATE

DEPLORABLE FIRE,

AT CHELMSFORD, ESSEX,

On Saturday Morning, March 19, 1808.

BY WHICH EVENT,

THE LIVES OF THREE UNFORTUNATE FEMALES

FELL

VICTIMS TO THE FLAMES,

Containing a full and true Detail of all the afflicting Circumstances,

COLLECTED FROM GENUINE AND AUTHENTIC ACCOUNTS,

EMBELLISHED BY

A GROUND PLAN OF THE TOWN,

WITH REFERENCES TO THE HOUSES DESTROYED

AND DAMAGED;

TO WHICH IS PREFIXED,

AN APPENDIX, CONTAINING THE SUBSEQUENT PROCEEDINGS,

WITH A LIST OF SUBSCRIBERS TO THE LIBERAL DONATIONS;

By a Witness of the fatal Catastrophe.

RESPECTFULLY INSCRIBED TO

THE INHABITANTS, NEIGHBOURHOOD, AND RELATIVES

OF THE MISERABLE SUFFERERS.

———

" In the Midst of Life we are in Death."—*Burial Service.*

———

PRINTED AT THE ESSEX PRESS;

Published, by R. H. Kelham, jun. at his Phœnix Circulating
Library, Chelmsford.

*Sold by Longman, Rees, and Co. and Vernor, Hood, & Sharpe, London;
Marshall and Robinson, Romford; Bush, Ipswich; Keymer, Colchester;
Rackham, Bury; Scruby, Ongar; Walter, Billericay; Draper, Maldon;
Rennison and Co. Southend; Tyler, Brentwood; and all Booksellers in
Town and Country.*

———

Price One Shilling.

Fire of 1808

The High Street, looking from the Shire Hall

Springfield Road, early 1900's

CHAPTER XII

mid-19th century
THE CATTLE FAIR

THE CATTLE FAIR was held in Fair Field in the upper part of Duke Street, which was then known as King's Street. Fair Field covered the area from the Railway Bridge and the viaduct and Viaduct Road to Coval Lane, which means that the Field is now occupied by Viaduct Road, the Eastern National Bus Station, Fairfield Road, the Civic Theatre, Chelmsford Public Library and the Municipal Offices.

The photograph on page 52 is of Duke Street or King's Street towards the end of the 19th century. Chelmsford Library is built on the site of the two cottages on the right-hand side of the road shown in the photograph. Part of Fair Field lies behind these cottages.

Fair Field was also the cricket and pleasure ground of Chelmsford, and was used for all special occasions such as fêtes, revels on the 5th November, and so on. It was, of course, also used for cricket matches, and on one occasion the ball was hit over the railway line; on another occasion the famous Dr.W.G. Grace played there.

The Burgess Well in the garden of No. 15 Fairfield Road, to which I have already referred, was the source of the water supply to the town in the 18th century.

The Poultry Market

The Poultry Market stood on the right-hand side of High Street, commencing from the point adjoining Bolingbroke & Wenley's Store to a point opposite Springfield Road corner where Marks & Spencer's Store is situated.

Stalls were erected on Market and Fair Days for the sale of all kinds of poultry (live and dead), vegetables and other farming products. Sometimes there was a fish stall.

CHAPTER XIII

SPRINGFIELD

BY THE Chelmsford Extension Order 1907, Springfield was added to the Borough of Chelmsford.

Muilman's *History of Essex,* published in 1770, records that Springfield 'lies about a mile north-east of the town of Chelmsford, upon a little eminence; the Chelmer serving as a boundary between the two parishes. The situation of this little village is pleasant and agreeable, commanding to the westward a pretty rural prospect, and on the other side, the great road, that leads to and from Colchester'. It is impossible to imagine it now.

The origin of the name is Campus Aquaticus, a field full of springs, but the name has been changed from time to time, sometimes Springafeld, at others Springinghefeld.

From the ancient records, we find that the chief part of the parish was formerly in the possession of one Alestan; but at the General Survey it was vested in Ralph Peverel, who held it by the name of Springafeld. At the same time the remaining part of it, which had been held by one Godric, was possessed by Robert Gernon, under the name of Springinghefeld.

It was at that time divided into the three following manors; Springfield Hall (with Dukes), Springfield Barnes, and Kewton, otherwise Cuton Hall.

The Manor of New Hall is likewise partly in the parish of Springfield.

Springfield Hall was the chief of the three manors; the Hall is still in existence, east of Lawn Lane.

From the 12th to the early 13th century, the estate was in the possession of a family surnamed de Bosevile or de Besevile, and then passed to the Godlingtons, Fermers and Olivers in succession, until by the late 15th century it became vested in Sir Thomas Tyrell of Springfield who held it at that time with Dukes or Deuks; Dukes still stands at the south-western corner of Springfield Green occupied by Essex County Council Education Department Central Area Office.

Part of the properties of Springfield by 1476 became vested in the Tyrell and Mildmay families, and Cuton Hall in Coggeshall Abbey, which at one time owned Springfield Barnes.

The church is of ancient structure, but was rebuilt in 1586. It is partly Norman. Oliver Goldsmith owned the house opposite the church.

Formerly there were two distinct rectors, two incumbents, patrons, and parsonage houses but, in 1753, at the request of Sir John Tyrell, then patron of both, the Bishop of London united them.

Trinity Church, in Trinity Road, was built in 1843. The original printed form of service which was used on the occasion of the laying of the first stone of Trinity Chapel (as it was then known) on 24th May 1842 may be seen at the church, together with the original notice of service giving various details of the names of the committee and others when the chapel was consecrated for use on 9th July 1843 by the Lord Bishop of London.

The church contains two fine old misericord seats in the sanctuary. They generally date back to the 14th or 15th centuries, and were stalls with tip-up wooden seats, with a projecting ledge on the under side, so that clergy could support themselves during the long services which required a great deal of standing. The ledges were known as 'misericords', and they often have elaborate carvings underneath which show not only scenes from the Bible but also grotesque figures of men and animals, the latter taken from semi mythical descriptions in popular medieval 'bestiaries' or books of beasts

One of the misericords at Holy Trinity Church is carved with a grotesque face, flanked with supporters, consisting of foliage and fruit — apparently grapes. The other is carved with a very fierce looking man (or it may represent a demon) battling with an equally ferocious-looking dragon, and is flanked with supporters also consisting of foliage and fruit, but differing from the other seat.

For many years there was also a fine old lacquer cased clock over the door at the west end of the church; recently the clock stopped and was taken down from the wall and now rests in the Hall adjoining the church. It is an 'antique' and the cost of repair would be prohibitive. The clock which bears the name of the maker is called an 'Act of Parliament' clock, commonly connected with Pitt's tax on clocks and watches; the Act was passed in the year 1797 but was repealed the following year on account of its unpopularity.

There are six almshouses in the parish of Springfield, four on the Green and two on the Waltham road; and the poor had a rent-charge on three fields called Great Perry-Field, Little Perry-Field and Millfield of £6.13s.4d., left by Robert Peaseley in the 16th century. Opposite Springfield Hall now stands

Perryfields School, a modern building, and thereby the 16th century becomes conjoined with the 20th.

Springfield Barnes was the next manor in the parish. Peter Muilman describes the Mansion House as 'agreeably placed near the banks of the river, at a little distance from the road from Chelmsford to Little Baddow, and appears to have been of some consequence'. This is a very vague description but George Sangster's map of 'The Manor of Barnes in Springfield, belonging to Mr. Alderman Porter' of the year 1755 shows the Manor House which is Springfield Barnes Farm House in Barnes Mill Lane. It is still in very good condition and occupied; the map shows the Mill Dam at the rear of the farm; it does not, however, show the Corn Mill which was adjoining the Dam for many years and which has now been refurbished, renovated and almost re-designed into a very attractive place of residence.

The family of Pese possessed the Springfield Barnes Manor House in the reign of Edward II, and that of his successor Edward III from whom it is traced into the noble families of Bohun and Bouchier. It went from them to Sir John Lodowic, who died in the 21st year of the reign of Henry IV. Later it became vested in Coggeshall Abbey and continued so vested until the Suppression. The monarch then granted it to Joanna de Bohun and others until, at the Dissolution, it was granted to William Mildmay, second son of Thomas Mildmay, of Moulsham Hall, and continued in the hands of that family until sold in the year 1650 to the Earl of Lindsey, when it came into the possession of Alderman Porter, whose executors sold it to Sir William Mildmay, which brought it back into that family.

After divers owners, it came in recent years into the ownership of the Marriage family and is now owned by the Fleming family.

Pease Hall (so named after the family of Pese) is now in the ownership of Capt. H. D'O Vigne, and lies equi-distant from Springfield Barnes and Cuton Hall. Speculation has it that Pease or Pese Hall was built for the youngest of the three sons, Thomas, William and John, Thomas having taken Springfield Barnes and William Cuton Hall.

Kewton, otherwise Cuton, Hall was the next Manor, which was formely part of New Hall.

Cuton Hall still stands on the original site and is occupied by Col. J.F. Cramphorn. Less than one hundred yards from Cramphorn's Garden Centre on the road to Sandford Mill you will find it tucked away at the end of a drive on the bend of the road.

In the reign of Edward III it was held by the name of Kyneton Hall by Thomas de Merk.

This manor later also became part of the endowment of Coggeshall Abbey and, at the Dissolution, Henry VIII granted it to Sir Thomas Seymour. After falling again into the monarch's hands, it was granted to John Pascall and eventually purchased by Robert Witham, a vintner of London, and later sold to James Ruck, a London banker. Since then it has continued to be vested in private hands.

As already mentioned, New Hall is partly in the parish of Springfield. It is now a Convent. It was used as a palace by Henry VIII and afterwards by Cromwell. (Cromwell paid 5s. for the Mansion and its estates.) It was noted for its long avenue of trees, nearly a mile in extent, which led to the Mansion. The old trees have long ago fallen to the axe but new ones have been planted.

On the southern side of the road, almost opposite New Hall, is Boreham House, now occupied by Fords. Up to the end part of the 19th century the park adjoining the house was well stocked with deer.

Springfield Place, lying at the eastern end of Springfield Church, also belonged to Robert Witham, Lord of the Manor of Cuton. Later it was purchased by John Strutt, and then passed from time to time into various other hands. It is now owned by Marconis and is used as a hostel for their students.

It is reputed to be haunted. Geoff Hales, a psychic and spirit-healer, encountered the phantom when he was working on the plumbing there in 1946. He said 'I saw a squat figure of a man move behind a large water tank in the attic'. Not getting a reply to his 'Good morning', he went behind the water tank to speak to the man but there was no sign of him. Later, an article appeared in *Essex Ghosts* by Wentworth Day, which gives a good description of the phantom and relates experiences of some of the people who have lived in the house over a number of years; and this description tallies with that of Geoff Hales.

In the year 1769 there was a Workhouse at the rear of Springfield Place. Described as a dwelling and two acres of land, which were given to the poor of the parish, the house was converted into 'a place for the reception of the most indigent amongst them'.

The area is now covered by houses, part of an estate

developed in recent years.

By the Chelmsford Extension Order 1907 Writtle was added to the Borough. It was always part of the Chelmsford Hundred, and is the largest parish in the county, including four hamlets — Oxney Green, Edney Common, Highwood and Cook's Mill Green. It is divided into four quarters — Town Quarter, Roman's Fee, Highwood and Bedell's End, and is 52 miles in circumference.

Writtle appears to have been a place of some importance from the earliest period of our history; and probably it was a sizeable town at the time Chelmsford was an obscure village. It has a strong claim to be regarded as the Caesaromagus — the name which is attributed to Chelmsford.

In later times, royalty had its residence there. The site of the palace of King John is believed to be a spot opposite Lordship Farm.

The principal stream of traffic flowed through Writtle from London to the coast until Bishop Maurice built the Stone Bridge.

It belonged in turn to King Harold, Edward the Confessor and William the Conqueror, and in later years to the Petre family, having been granted to Sir William Petre by Queen Mary in the 16th century. It was a market town and has a charter for a fair on Whit Monday and 10th October.

The present church was completed early in the 13th century, sometime between 1230—50. It was extensively damaged by fire in March 1974 and the church, as it now stands, is the result of restoration painstakingly researched and carried out over many months.

A church has existed in Writtle from at least early Norman times, since there is mention of a church and a priest in the Domesday Survey of the manor; and it is more than probable that a church existed prior to that.

CHAPTER XIV

THE 18th AND 19th CENTURIES

FROM THE middle of the 18th century to the end of the 19th century, many changes and much development took place in the town. In 1724 the *Essex Chronicle* was launched; cost 2½d. a copy.

Following the Bill for the Navigation of the Chelmer in 1765, the canal basin was first opened in 1797 and was used for the transport of timber and coal; but the town was still mainly concerned with its market, its inns, cornmills, breweries and tanneries.

Cromptons commenced business in 1878, Hoffmanns in 1899 and Marconi's in 1900. A few years previously, however, Fell Christy commenced business in a small shop in Broomfield Road; that was in 1858. His speciality was machinery for wind and water mills. By 1883 his business had developed into an Electrical and Engineering Works — a large concern known as 'Christy Brothers'.

During the same period the town's administrative importance was increasing, and in 1888 it was, of course, incorporated as a Borough. It was in that year there occurred the Great Flood of Chelmsford. This was in the closing days of July and the opening days of August of that year. Destructive storms and disastrous floods, with an abnormally low temperature, supplanted the usual dry, hot weather.

The destruction of immense crops of grain caused great havoc, bridges broken down, houses and public buildings destroyed; cattle killed by lightning and drowned by floods.

The disaster occurred between the Wednesday night and Thursday morning, which was preceded on the Monday by heavy storms of thunder and lightning. Late on Wednesday there was another violent thunder storm.

The accumulation of the overflow from the various watersheds raised the already swollen streams to such a degree that they overflowed their banks; and great destruction was inevitable.

Writtle Street, London Road, High Street, Moulsham Street and Baddow Road were all completely under water. The people living in the houses in these roads were in great fear of their lives.

Captain Showers (the Chief Constable) and Raglan

Somerset (his Deputy) and a strong force of officers, mounted and on foot, were called up.

The bridge in London Road gave way at 8 a.m. and the flooding swept along London Road and through the Friars, into Moulsham Street and Mildmay Road. It swept over Fulcher's Market Garden, wrecking his crops at one fell swoop.

Another swift current carried all before it between the river and Barrack Square, razing the river wall, rushing out by the Co-op Stores and along Baddow Road to join the former stream which found its way down Goldlay Road, the fields of Charles Harrison Gray at Goldlay House together with the Baddow Meads forming a vast sea of water, with the intervening Baddow Road lost to sight.

Houses and basements were flooded; every conceivable object could be seen floating down the river. Where the waters swirled round like so many whirlpools on the Meads behind the Kings Head, and further towards Navigation Road, a bedstead, sofa, hen coops, water butts, oil casks, &c. were dancing about as if mockingly inviting sufferers to pay a visit and commence the work of identification.

To get from one part of the town to the other, pedestrians had either to pass through deep water on foot or be taken in vehicles supplied by local tradesmen. Many a man with a pony and trap made a small fortune.

The High Street was under water. The Can overflowed; and the ever-widening stream reached clean through the centre of the town, knocking down brick walls, filling up the cellars, passing through houses, in one door and out of the other, in its mad course to the Blackwater.

At one time, the whole area from the Post Office to Hall Street was covered with water.

Water poured through the Queen's Head Yard, bearing on its surface water butts, crates and the like. A large piano was also seen floating amongst the flotsam and jetsam.

By the middle of the day the water subsided, leaving the High Street free for traffic, and the houses filled with dirty water.

The ground floors were choked up with mud and hundreds of pounds worth of damage had been done in the High Street alone.

Bolingbroke's cellar was filled with valuable warehoused goods, most of which were salvaged.

Singers' Sewing Machines' cellar was filled with machines

which were all very badly damaged. (Singers' was on part of the site of the present Marks & Spencers.)

At the Queen's Head two horses and a donkey were saved from the flood; the donkey was head and ears only above the water.

The cellar of Collins & Sons (the China Shop) was stored with goods, some of which rose to the surface of the water, filled, and then sank with a crash. Their losses must have been heavy.

The photograph on page 85 shows the China Shop at that time. Later, the business was transferred to Springfield Road corner and continued there until the 1930's. The building was then redeveloped and taken over by the Fifty Shilling Tailors. It was only recently reconstructed and occupied by Dorothy Perkins.

You will see in the photograph 'Goss China' advertised over the front of the shop. 'Goss' china (or heraldic china) was beloved of many people 50 to 60 years ago — they used it to form collections and show it off in cabinets. It was usually decorated with arms of boroughs and municipalities.

J.G. Bonds' Moulsham Street Store, lost a great deal of drapery as a result of the flood. The store (now known as 'Debenhams') was not where it is now; it was next to the 'Cross Keys' public house (the site on which the Regent Theatre was subsequently built).

Adjoining Bonds' was the basket maker, S.B. Turner; he had a cellar full of baskets, most of which were spoiled beyond recall. Turner's basket-making business was in existence until round about the beginning of the Second World War.

Barrels of liquor were afloat in the cellar of the Cross Keys which, incidentally, was demolished in 1912 to make way for the erection of the Regent Theatre. (See the photograph on page 90.)

Many other inns shared the same fate.

The water began to enter New London Road, above the Iron Bridge, before 5 o'clock when it forced an opening from the meadows through the Infirmary grounds; the wall dividing the Infirmary from the adjoining property collapsed, and the stream by this time had assumed a force which threatened to carry all before it.

The people living in the neighbourhood were called up by the police, and at half-past five a Miss Annette Coleman, at London Road Iron Works (then opposite the Infirmary), waded through the water to the foundry bell, by which she summoned the men to the premises. They arrived in time to take up the carpets before the water rushed in.

Soon, chairs, tables and stools were seen floating about in hopeless confusion.

The occupants of the houses on the Institute side of London Road were unable to save anything at all.

The water poured through the Infirmary gates, crossed the road, out into the Friars, four feet deep.

The houses near the Bridge were all flooded; the water in each case all but reached the ceilings.

The caretaker of the Congregational Church was saved from drowning by climbing through the window of the church.

In London Road below the bridge, i.e. from the bridge to the High Street, the houses in the vicinity of the bridge were flooded to a depth varying from two to seven feet.

Museum Terrace (then opposite Marks & Spencer's present store) from the house of a Dr. Down, whose residence adjoined the river, to the livery stables of Mr. Bushell, was all under water, from floor to ceiling; the gardens looked like a great lake.

A great willow tree was washed into the river and became irremoveably fixed athwart the bridge, on the Institute side of it. Efforts were made to remove it without success; and the bridge, which had been erected 540 years before, crashed at 8 o'clock.

The Baptist Chapel (adjoining the Hospital) and then recently renovated, suffered considerable damage. Hymn books, cushions and hassocks, together with furniture and a harmonium, were swept away.

Occupants of houses in the Friars were unable to leave their houses on account of the strength of the current and, in order that some might obtain breakfast, ropes were thrown from the Old Friars Coffee Tavern to the houses on the opposite side of the road and, along the ropes, baskets containing food and tea and coffee were drawn.

Water entered the British School and caused great damage; water rushed from the Friars to Barrack Square and the river and carried away 20 yards of the river wall, thereby increasing the volume of water into the roads adjoining.

Gallant rescues were made. One policeman, P.C. Watcham, waded breast-deep in water; he swam and waded until he reached the front of the house; by the aid of a linen line he rescued Mrs. Thorn and her family.

Pigs, looking like bladders, were floating in New Writtle Street; they were all saved.

From Baddow Road corner to the Army & Navy Inn, it was one swiftly flowing stream, the deepest part being near Goldlay Road. At one cottage in Goldlay Road, a baby was planted on the middle of a table while her mother plied her broom to keep out the water.

A temporary bridge was erected over the river in London Road and plans prepared for the erection subsequently of a permanent bridge — the present one.

Trains in the Springfield cutting were stranded; there was a sheet of water half a mile long which prevented the movement of any railway stock. Witham Station was flooded; and part of the Kelvedon line.

Bad as this all sounds, a flood of greater severity descended upon the town on 24th June 1824; I have not been able to obtain details of this disaster but the record I found said that 'the floods rose as high as the present premises of London & County Bank' and poured from the river into the High Street from what was then known as Theatre Yard — a site which now marks the entrance to London Road. On that occasion people rowed boats along High Street to Moulsham.

The floods then extended to Writtle, Widford and Maldon.

The greatest sufferers in the town then were the tradesmen in the three principal streets.

* * * * * * * *

The *Essex Weekly News* of 21st January 1881 on page 8 records another disaster which hit the town; this was the great snowstorm in Essex.

Sharp frosts and keen winds had been followed by one of the heaviest downfalls of snow that had been known in Essex within living memory. Snow, accompanied by a boisterous, easterly wind, commenced to fall at about 11 in the morning and continued to snow and blow without ceasing until close upon midnight, the result being that before evening the roads in and around the town were choked and blocked by snow, especially where it had been blown by the wind into huge drifts, and traffic was almost entirely suspended, the streets and roads deserted, and in several instances considerable damage was done to property. Driven hither and thither by the boisterous wind, the snow and sleet penetrated into houses and workshops and caused damage. Almost all work was suspended after 12 noon.

At about two o'clock the hurricane was at its height, the force of the wind so great that at times it was impossible to face it. By this time the streets were full of snow, which in some parts had drifted into hugh heaps three or four feet deep. Hour after hour the downfall continued, until the roads were practically impassable.

The Rochford coach, which had started its return journey from Chelmsford between three and four o'clock, had proceeded some distance along Baddow Road, when it found the way so blocked with snow that it was impossible to continue. The coachman was obliged to turn back and, with several passengers, found lodgings in the town for the night. At nearly all the schools in the town, work was suspended during the afternoon and, in the case of children living at a little distance from the town, anxious endeavours were made to get them safely home before matters got worse. A scene such as this had never before been witnessed, while in the roads leading into the town even a worse state of things prevailed; Springfield and Baddow Roads were six feet deep in snow. A host of mishaps were reported. At Galleywood, two drays, a wagon and a brougham sunk into such a depth of snow that it was deemed advisable to release the horses, which was done after a great deal of trouble. Serious delays occurred on the railway, and postal services were completely disorganised.

A woman narrowly escaped perishing in the snow in Baddow Road; her cries were heard and she was found up to her waist in snow and in a very exhausted condition; she was taken to the Army & Navy Inn, nearby, where restoratives were administered. She was warned not to continue on her journey home at Slade's Lane, Baddow Road, but she insisted. She was, once again, embedded in a snow drift, but was found by her husband who was out looking for her. He managed to get her home safely.

There were incidents of children being caught in the snow. One small boy who wandered about for hours at Danbury was eventually found in an exhausted state and taken in and cared for until his parents, frantic for his safety by this time, had been contacted.

Another case was of two little girls named Clarke and Chipperfield, aged 12 and 14 years, who were going home from Springfield School towards Brook-end, when they became embedded in the snow in the lane contiguous to Springfield Prison. This was, of course, Sandford Road. They were eventually discovered, exhausted, and taken to the Police Station, nearby. Here they remained for about three hours when, hearing of no enquiry about them, it was decided to take them home. A Sergt. Gifford volunteered to make the attempt but after vainly endeavouring to force a passage through the heavy drift for over two hours, he lodged them at the house of a woman named Willis. On the following day the little girls were conveyed to their homes in a cart.

As soon as the downfall ceased, which was about midnight, a large force of men were employed in clearing the roads of snow; in some places the drifts were as high as nine feet. The snow was carted 'to the field at the back of the new Market Place' — this was, of course, the Recreation Ground, now known as Central Park.

Collins & Sons, the China Shop

CHAPTER XV

THE FIRST WORLD WAR

CHELMSFORD in the year 1914 was not much more than a large market town; there was very little housing or other development beyond Broomfield Road corner in the north or beyond Oaklands Park in the south and Marriage's Mill in Baddow Road in the east.

Almost without exception the streets were considerably narrower than at present.

The photograph on page 89 shows Broomfield Road corner and the old Temperance Hotel, the site of which is now occupied by Barclays Bank; the building is structurally the same, the inside only having been altered. The clump of trees on the left is the site of the Pavilion Cinema which was built in 1927.

The last houses in Springfield Street were on the site of the Leys; beyond that — open fields on each side of a narrow country road leading to Boreham and Witham*.

Springfield Street has changed considerably; the small houses and cottages standing at that time have all been demolished and modern houses erected in their stead. The two public houses, the Plough and the Endeavour, however, have remained; they have stood there for many years and look the same as they did 40 years ago.

From Timson's Lane to Bishop's Court many changes have taken place; most of the houses are modern ones built on the sites of older houses and cottages. Similarly, from Stump Lane to Arbour Lane, most of the old mansions have been demolished and, on the sites of those mansions and grounds, have been built Llewellyn Close and Dalrymple Close and Regency Close.

Pump Lane was a narrow, winding country lane boasting one small farm and a cottage as far as the eye could see in the direction of Broomfield. The fields on the left-hand side of the lane going towards Broomfield were used as an airfield during the 1914—18 war.

Old Court Road was built between the two wars; the land on which it was developed as far as Arbour Lane was a paddock used for horse riding and jumping.

Springfield Hill from Arbour Lane to Victoria Road was 'the village', and the main shopping area of Springfield. The

---

* Springfield Lyons, then occupied by Major Magor, the cottages and the White Hart Inn, were at that time outside the Chelmsford boundary.

Hill consisted of a row of small shops on the right-hand side from the top of the Hill opposite the entrance to the Church-yard to the bottom of the Hill, and on the other side, small cottages from the Churchyard entrance to half-way down the Hill. Next to the cottages was a Bakery and a small General shop, and then more houses as far as Trinity Road. The shops have changed hands from time to time and most of them have been modernised, but the cottages have been demolished and a row of almshouses built in their stead.

Springfield Towers, the only attractive building in the neighbourhood, is situate off the main road and between there and Rabbit's Walk. The towers of the mansion can still be seen from Springfield Road; the house and grounds have now been developed as a housing estate reaching to Rabbit's Walk opposite the railway line.

The general aspect of this part of Springfield Road has changed little.

At the bottom of the Hill was a butcher, a grocer, a news-agent, a public house (The Oddfellows Arms), a laundry and a row of small terrace houses; a petrol Service Station now occupies the site of the laundry and the cottages. The Oddfellows Arms, however, remains a link with the past. Between there and Meadowside was a row of houses, still standing, together with the Essex Arms public house on the corner of St. Anne's Place. This public house is dilapidated, shuttered and empty. For many years the two public houses, The Oddfellows Arms and The Essex Arms, were establishments patronised considerably by local inhabitants, and were centres of gay and jovial activity — mostly noisy, sometimes scenes of fighting in the summer evenings when the pea pickers were in the vicinity.

Between Trinity Road and Weight Road very little struc-tural change has taken place since 1914. A confectioner's shop stood on the corner of Trinity Road and next to it was a Fishmonger.

These small shops on the Hill were all typical, small country shops. But if you wanted really nice, high-class fruit you would go to Miss Byford's shop adjoining the Fishmonger's. The prices were high but the fruit good and worth the extra money.

A Hairdresser's Salon stood between Miss Byford's and the Three Cups public house. This establishment has not altered one iota over the years. Immediately opposite is Victoria Road and the Anglian Regional Water Authority's office, but it was many years before Victoria Road came into being.

A large country house stood where the Anglian Regional Authority's Divisional Office now stands, and adjoining it was a plot of land having a frontage to Springfield Road of 100 feet or thereabouts through which ran a narrow lane leading to Bradridge's Mill and the ford across the river; the bridge now crossing the river covers the site of the old ford. Beyond this plot to the north were allotment gardens reaching to the river.

There was a narrow wooden bridge across the river which led to the old Victoria Road, which commenced almost at the corner of Regina Road, near the entrance to the Car Park. This path was only a few feet above the level of the fields on either side but, because of flooding in the winter months, the height of the path was raised to approximately the level of the present road. The site of the Cattle Market and row of shops adjoining Victoria Road was pasture land the level of which was some 10 feet below the level of the present road.

The fields through which Victoria Road runs was known as 'Cups Fields' (originally part of Tunman Mead) and probably belonged to the owner of the Three Cups, a man named Frederick Weight. As the public house adjoins Weight Road it is possible he was concerned in the development of the road.

Adjoining Weight Road is Boswells House, and the photograph on page 72 shows Boswells and the Three Cups and the entrance to the country house ("Shrublands") on which the Anglian Water Authority's office stands.

The land within the curtilege of Boswells in 1914 extended to Navigation Road, and was almost all orchard; it was put up for auction in 1918 and was later developed as it is now, having changed little in the intervening years.

The remainder of Springfield Road was subjected to very little change until recent years; within the past decade most of the large houses have been demolished and modern buildings erected on the sites.

The area recently occupied by the Petrol Station on Horsepond Bridge was originally the site of the Wesleyan Chapel erected there in 1843 in lieu of a smaller chapel built in 1813 and later used as a school. As I have mentioned earlier, a new Chapel was built in 1847 for the Wesleyan Chapel on the site now occupied by Caters' Stores. After the Wesleyan Chapel moved to High Street the building on Horsepond Bridge was used successively as a Motor Garage and Show Rooms.

Horsepond Bridge is so called because horses were watered

The Windmill Inn, Moulsham Street

Broomfield Road corner at the turn of the century

The Half Moon, c.1895

The Cross Keys, early 1900's

Tindal Square c. 1876

Mʀꜱ. DRUMMOND & SUFFRAGETTES IN PRISON DRESS.

Mrs. Drummond and Suffragettes in front of the Corn Exchange

91

The High Street 1876

The Procession carrying the Charter

there; the area covered by the pond is now filled in, and concreted and used by Brown & Son Limited.

Adjoining the Petrol Filling Station was a field stretching beyond the river to the Swimming Baths and Victoria Road; the whole field on both sides of the river was continuously flooded during the winter months, and the cottages and shops between the bridge and the Two Brewers were always awash when the floods broke over the level of the road. It was a pitiful sight to see the occupiers of the cottages bailing out the flood waters from their habitations and salvaging what furniture they could when the water subsided.

There was great activity at the bridge on the morning of the outbreak of the 1914 war, when the Essex Yeomanry mustered there prior to moving off to the Railway Station to embark for France. Reports in the *Essex Weekly News* and the *Essex Chronicle* now make very interesting reading. The Essex Infantry Brigade was at camp at Clacton on the day of the outbreak of war for its annual training. There were greater numbers there that year, as a bounty of £1 per man per day had been offered to anyone who stayed at camp for 15 days. None of them returned home from camp as they had anticipated; they were simply moved from the camp to the various regiments to make up their strengths. This was all in accordance with a previously planned arrangement made in readiness for such an emergency. In addition, horses were requisitioned; this did not include farm horses, as these would have been needed on the farms. All reservists were called to the colours.

All officers of the Territorial Infantry Brigade who had not attended camp at Clacton received orders to join the Brigade at once.

All men in the Metropolitan Police on leave were recalled; cyclists of the Braintree section of the Cyclists Corps connected with the Essex Territorials received orders from their Headquarters at Colchester to proceed there forthwith.

Naval aeroplanes patrolled the coast and the Thames Estuary.

Springfield Road at Horsepond Bridge in 1914 was narrower than at present, and the bridge was shorter and made of old-fashioned brickwork; a small tributary of the river Chelmer ran from the direction of Debenham's Car Park along the side of the field next to the bridge, underneath the bridge to the pond, thence through what is now Brown & Son Ltd.'s yard, behind Stone House and the shop premises adjoining the house, and subsequently joined the Chelmer south of the Iron Bridge further along Springfield Road. The small tributary has now been cut off by the Anglian Water Authority, and it can be seen how this has been done by taking a look at the bridge from Debenham's Car Park; there is no sign of the tributary, which was filled in and concreted about 10 years ago.

The river Chelmer rises at Henham and runs south east by Thaxted, Dunmow and Little Waltham, passes through Chelmsford, and, joining the Can, falls into the sea between Foulness and Burnham.

The area of land bounded by the tributary on the east which flows under Horsepond Bridge and the main river Chelmer flowing under the Iron Bridge in Springfield Road was an island. It is known as Mesopotamia Island to this day.

'Tradition informs us,' says Thomas Wright in his *History of Essex*, published in 1836, 'that, so far back as the memory of man runneth, it has been the custom, that on the death of an Essex member, or when the great council of the nation has been dissolved, and a regeneration of their collective wisdom has taken place, the island of Mesopotamia should also exercise the elective franchise.'

Before the day of the election, the mayor of this peculiar jurisdiction issued a proclamation, giving notice that he would proceed to the election of a representative or representatives for the island of Mesopotamia; and after giving the names of the candidates, who were always celebrated or dignified characters, he proceeded to state that the election would take place on a certain appointed day, at 12 o'clock, upon the island, opposite the Duke's Head Inn, 'where every accommodation will be provided for the candidates and their friends'.

As the election proceeded, the candidates were seen parading the streets on horseback, each attended by a page; a band of music headed the procession, which usually made a stand opposite the inn where some of the real candidates for the county representation were stationed, and the speeches made on those occasions seldom failed to produce a great deal of humour, highly gratifying to the assembled crowd.

When the poll terminated, the successful candidates were immediately chaired, and borne on men's shoulders through the crowded streets of Chelmsford. By the charter of the island it is provided that at the conclusion of the ceremony they shall be conducted to the river and undergo the ceremony of submersion; after which, and the tearing of the chair to pieces, the important business of the day closes. The Mesopotamia election was always held on the island, between the two bridges, a day or two after the election of a member or members for the county. By an abuse of the established custom of this ancient corporation, the losing, as well as the successful, candidates were bathed in 'the stream of the Chelmer'.

Whether the 'stream of the Chelmer' meant the tributary leading to the pond, or whether it was the Chelmer itself is not clear. The report ends as follows: 'But it is doubted by the better informed of the members, that this ceremony was originally considered as honorary, and by no means intended for those who had not been so fortunate as to have become the favourites of the people.'

* * * * * * * *

The entrance to Debenham's Car Park and the next door premises in 1914 was then known as Dukes Head Yard and The Rosebery Yard; No. 211 Springfield Road in Dukes Head Yard was then occupied by Archers, the Banana Wholesalers but, prior to that, it was occupied by three men, A.J. Burls, Charles Hawkes and Albert William Hawkes, trading as 'Hawkes Bros.', wholesale confectioners, who manufactured their confectionery in the buildings in the Yard. They were then in a small way of business and continued in partnership there until 1911 when they moved to premises in New Street, now occupied partly by the new Police Headquarters. There they flourished, and subsequently became the well-known 'Hawkes Bros. Ltd.', the East Anglian Confectionery Company. The premises which they took over in New Street in 1911 had been occupied by a man named Lees, a wholesale confectioner, who had employed the three partners of Hawkes Bros. some years before. Lees went bankrupt, and the three partners took over the premises of their old employer — one of the many success stories of Chelmsford businesses. They had the first trade motor vehicle in the Town; that was in 1912.

Between Dukes Head Yard and the Iron Bridge was a row of shops including a Drapers and a small Hardware merchant, the latter abutting immediately upon the bridge. On the opposite side was the Empire Cinema which was built during the First World War. Beyond the bridge on the same side as the cinema was an old established coach-makers, Munnions, with small, beautifully-made models of coaches and carriages on display which could be seen through the main window.

Adjoining the coach-makers in succession was a chemist, a small dairy, an antique shop and a fish shop. Opposite the row of shops was, and still is, the office and yard of Gray & Sons, the Brewers. It is all scheduled for redevelopment; this will be a great improvement to a very dismal area of Chelmsford.

Adjoining the fish shop was a low archway leading into a slum area called 'French's Square' — now demolished — and is occupied partly by the entrance to the Car Park and partly by the Woolworth building.

The remainder of the site occupied by Woolworths was a Tailor's, a Barber's shop, and Collins, the Glassware and China shop which extended to the corner of Springfield Road, now taken over by Dorothy Perkins. Collins' China shop was formerly carried on in High Street.

The print on page 29 showing the Post Office in 1762 on the corner of Springfield Road (then known as Colchester and Harwich Road) reveals that the general outline of High Street has not altered materially; the line of frontage of the shops from Springfield Road to London Road is approximately the same; and the building in the top left-hand corner is surely the site occupied by Lloyds Bank. Compare this view with the photograph on page 69 showing the Conduit; the photograph shows the Shire Hall as we know it. The old Shire Hall can be seen in the print but it is partly obscured by the sign of the Red Lion.

According to the Survey of Chelmsford of 1591 the old Shire Hall was in existence at that time but was replaced by the existing building in 1790.

The view of High Street on page 30 shows a Post Office on the left-hand side of the street just beyond the lamp post; the words 'Post Office' are very faint but they can be discerned. A lady wearing a long flowing black skirt and a white garment or shawl is looking into the window. The Post Office was subsequently moved to the building between Bank Chambers and Barclays Bank, but is, of course, now on the corner of Market Road, part of Chancellor Hall. I doubt whether the drawing of the High Street showing the Post Office on the left-hand side of the street is drawn to scale, as almost opposite the Post Office is shown the *Essex Weekly News* building; in fact, the old Post Office stood on the site occupied by K. Shoes, and the building opposite is the southern end of Debenhams. It may be that at that time the Debenham site was the newspaper office,

96

but in living memory the *Essex Weekly News* building was further along the street immediately adjoining Debenhams on the north. Debenhams, of course, took over the business of Bonds.

As recently as the 1920's J.G. Bond was a one-man business with premises having a frontage of not more than 30 to 35 feet; the business developed in the 1920's and 1930's and acquired the adjoining property up to the point immediately adjoining the old site of *Essex Weekly News,* the proprietor of which was Sidney Taylor, a past mayor of the town. In the inter-war years a restaurant was opened on the first floor of Bond's, and this was a popular meeting place for local people for many years, particularly on a Saturday morning. During the week when the local Operatic Society 'took over' the Regent Theatre for their annual production, many of the leading ladies and gentlemen, who often took a week of their annual holiday that week, would be seen besporting themselves during the mornings in the restaurant, expecting and receiving the congratulations of the staff and friends on their histrionic prowess. Below them, the main window of the central part of the premises displayed a host of photographs of scenes from the current production for all and sundry to see and comment upon. Chelmsford then was not the large city of today; most people knew everyone else and the annual Operatic Society's production was one of the events of the year.

Another meeting place for local people before Bond's Restaurant came into being was the delightful cakeshop-cum-teashop situate between Green's, the Clothiers, and Bond's, at No. 32 High Street. It was owned by the Misses Hicks, two maiden ladies. It was an old established business and savoured of the Victorian period; it was demolished and the site redeveloped in 1932. That was partly on the site of Debenham's and partly on the site lately occupied by Marks & Spencer.

CHAPTER XVI

THE SHOOTING DOWN OF THE L.32

DURING THE 1914—1918 war a number of large open areas of the countryside were requisitioned for airfields — training and operational. Sandford Road was the site of one training station, Pump Lane, Springfield, was another, and an operational airfield at Broomfield. These airfields drew the enemy aircraft, Zeppelins and aeroplanes. A number of enemy aircraft were shot down in the area; but the most memorable incident for Chelmsford was the shooting down of the Zeppelin, the L.32, by Second Lieutenant F. Sowrey who was patrolling the area in his aircraft on the 3rd September 1916 just before 1 a.m. In his report he says:

'At 12.45 a.m. I noticed an enemy airship in an easterly direction. I at once made in this direction and maoeuvred into a position underneath. The airship was well lighted by search-lights, but there was no sign of any gunfire. I could distinctly see the propellers revolving, and the airship was manoeuvring to avoid the searchlight beams. I fired at it. The first two drums of ammunition had apparently no effect, but the third one caused the envelope to catch fire in several places; in the centre and front . . . . . I watched the burning airship strike the ground and then proceeded to find my flares.'

The Zeppelin fell to the ground in flames at Snail's Hall Farm, Great Burstead. Its journey to earth seemed painfully slow, and a number of objects were seen to fall from the airship. All on board perished, and the wreckage burned for nearly an hour. The remains of the bodies of the crew were buried in the churchyard at Great Burstead Church, but were disinterred some years ago and taken back to Germany for re-burial.

CHAPTER XVII

THE TWENTIES

CHELMSFORD did not develop or change physically to any extent until after the end of the First World War.

The local business men, many of whom, from time to time, members of the Town Council, were responsible for certain developments and improvements; several of them served the office of Mayor, some of them more than once. But the people who were concerned mostly in the building development and the development of estates for building purposes were not members of the Town Council, as I will explain later.

Well-known families living in and around Chelmsford such as the Mildmays and Strutts and the owners of Oaklands, Moulsham Hall and Hylands, Broomfield Lodge and Broomfield Hall and many others soon realised after the First World War that their estates were attracting the attention of builders and estate developers; and during the inter-war years of 1919 and 1939 most of the estates were, in fact, sold for these purposes.

High taxation after the First World War proved burdensome to many of the old, theretofore wealthy landed gentry; and it proved increasingly difficult to obtain staff, both domestic and outdoor, to work for them. The result was that the estates were one by one put up for auction or sold by private treaty. Local Auctioneers and Estate Agents were soon 'in the money'. Alfred Darby & Co. and Fred Taylor & Co. were the two main firms and neither firm appeared to be anything but flourishing. Later, other firms appeared on the Chelmsford scene, Strutt & Parker being one. They have continued to flourish and, in due course, Alfred Darby & Co. became merged with and swallowed up by them.

Immediately after the First World War, however, the two main firms of Auctioneers, were Alfred Darby & Co. and Fred Taylor & Co. and theirs were the names to be seen on all the Particulars of Sale and on all the Sale Notices seen on the hoardings in the Town. Solicitors were, of course, necessary for all transactions of real estate — and most firms of Solicitors were hives of industry, and many of them found it necessary either to extend their premises or move to larger ones.

The 1920's was not an era of Building Societies; mortgages for small house purchases were not so easily available as they are nowadays. The Oddfellows Friendly Society was one source of funds for mortgages but it was a limited one. Many thrifty people who had a few hundred pounds to invest took up this means of investment.

It was possible to purchase a cottage or small house for, say, £250, and a 'Three up and three down' for £450 or £500; and to invest in real estate always was and still is sound economics. The trouble was that with a private mortgage the mortgagee could always call in his mortgage on giving three months' notice or on payment of three months' interest, which then was usually not more than 5%. There were few (if any) long-term mortgages available such as those now offered by Building Societies. Chelmsford & Essex Building & Investment Society was established in 1845 but they do not appear to have developed to any great extent. The Banks made loans to customers for house purchase but these loans were usually short-term loans, except perhaps for members of their staffs who had the benefit of a low rate of interest on their loans anyway. When a private mortgagee called in his loan there was frequently difficulty finding someone else who would take over the mortgage; this is not a hazard with modern Building Societies.

Groups of local business men invested money in private mortgages of the nature I have just mentioned; these men were from various trades and professions — the law, shopkeepers, farmers, builders etc. They all did remarkably well; they were men of keen business and, but for the service they rendered (to their own profit, 'tis true!), many people would not have been able to own their own houses at that time.

These groups were well organised; there was a great deal of professional jealousy in the town as a result of the undoubted success of their undertakings, as one after another of the large family estates were taken over by this coterie of men. The local people jokingly referred to them as 'The Forty Thieves'.

It was due to the operations of these men that Chelmsford developed in the inter-war years. All the land forming part of the Oaklands Estate and Moulsham Lodge Estate was purchased by them and cut up as building estates.

Vicarage Road was extended into Longstomps Avenue, and the making of the roads adjoining Vicarage Road and Longstomps followed.

The A12 from Widford (parts of Rollestons Farm) and Princes Road and Chelmer Road — all part of the A12 — were built.

Moulsham School was also part of Moulsham Lodge Estate. Other parts became Bruce Grove, Stewart Road, Burns Crescent, Hillside Grove and Moulsham Drive and Lynmouth Avenue, and all the roads in those areas.

The operations of the 'Forty Thieves' extended along Galleywood Road into the village where estates have been developed in Deadman's Lane and Watchhouse Lane, and other areas in the vicinity.

Other parts of the town also came into their orbit; First, Second, Third, Fourth, Fifth, Sixth and Seventh Avenues, and on the other side of the road at Broomfield, Patching Hall Estate.

Whatever remarks were made facetiously about the 'Forty Thieves', this coterie of men served an important function at the time, and there are many families in Chelmsford and the surrounding district whose now flourishing businesses owe their origin to their financial help. Great characters, some of them, and very much part of the scene of Chelmsford. You would see them all at around 4 o'clock on a Friday afternoon at the Sales at the Corn Exchange — now demolished and part of Chancellor Hall.

CHAPTER XVIII

HIGH STREET IN THE 1920's

AS YOU WILL see from the prints of Chelmsford in previous centuries, even as late as 1880, the surface of High Street was gravelled; more recently, it was surfaced with wooden blocks, which were tarred and sanded over. It was a very effective-looking surface too, and extremely good. The trouble arose when the river Chelmer and the river Can overflowed in times of heavy rainfall during the winter, and especially when there had been a heavy fall of snow in the district; the snow melted, and the rivers and streams, all flowing into the two main rivers, could not be contained. This resulted in sewers overflowing and flooding into the town. Flooding has always been a hazard here.

Springfield Road, at each end of Horsepond Bridge, was completely submerged almost as far as Navigation Road in one direction and as far as the Iron Bridge in the other. The fields lying between the Horsepond Bridge and the Swimming Bath on one side, and Wray & Fuller's yard on the other, were also under water. Further afield, in Baddow Road, in the area between Goldlay Road and Lady Lane, the road was impassable. It is difficult to picture Baddow Road at that time, as the Ring Road has transformed the area. But the road was narrow and low-lying — at least two feet below the level of the river bank — which was separated from the road by an area covered by grass which varied from approximately 30 feet opposite Goldlay Road to up to 60 feet opposite Lynmouth Avenue.

In addition, and far more serious, was the effect of the flooding on the shops in High Street; the rivers flowed and still flow through the town and, in the case of the river Can, beneath the High Street at the Stone Bridge, adjoining Body's, the Chemist's.

The Chelmer flows beneath the Iron Bridge in Springfield Road between the various properties owned by Debenham's on one side, into the Baddow Meads, passing the Odeon Cinema and other buildings, and Gray & Sons, the Brewers, on the other. In those early days neither Bond's nor Debenham's were owners of the property adjoining the river Chelmer — Dukes Head Yard and Rosebery Yard occupied the whole site.

The pressure of the flood waters forced up manhole covers and drain tops all over the town, and also the wooden blocks of the surface of the High Street. This caused great chaos and damage. Most of the main roads and streets were impassable.

Eventually, the Essex River Board (now having developed into the Essex Division Anglian Water Authority) dealt with the situation very effectively by its work on the two rivers. But before flooding was an annual anticipation. Great credit is due to the work of this Authority.

Nicolas Tindal

103

CHAPTER XIX

KRUSCHEN

AFTER THE First World War, Chelmsford entered a new phase. The expansion of industries carried on by Hoffmanns, Cromptons and Marconi's resulted in the employment of greater numbers of men and women; this in turn called for the building of more houses. This all ushered in a period of prosperity; the shopkeepers prospered, and whenever the opportunity arose they extended their premises and increased the number of employees. The shopkeeping fraternity of the town in those days were private and family concerns. Later, gradually the big combines and business houses moved in, buying up some of the businesses as and when they came on to the market. The new owners found it necessary to improve the look of their premises to compete with local custom; but the improvements did not at that time include sites other than those in the main thorough-fares, and most of the side streets remained unaffected. Springfield Road, as I have pointed out, was one of the side streets, despite the fact that it was part of the main route from London to the Coast.

The By-Pass from Widford to Springfield (Princes Road) was not built until 1932, and all traffic through the town from all directions came by way of London Road and Moulsham Street and High Street into Springfield Road to the Coast.

Driving vehicles from Springfield Road into High Street and vice versa always presented a hazard because of the narrow-ness of the road (as, in fact, it does now), and although the Conduit served a purpose by helping to divide the traffic travelling along the High Street, there was often chaos at this corner at weekends during the summer months with a tremen-dously large volume of traffic travelling to and from the Coast. The congestion which ensued at these times and the frustrations of some of the policemen on point duty fascinated the local inhabitants who would stand in groups for hours on end on a Saturday or Sunday evening watching the passing scene.

A policeman was, of course, always on point duty at Springfield Road corner; and each did his best to regulate the traffic. During normal hours this was not a particularly diffi-cult operation; weekends were the times which presented the problems. No one policeman was any better than another — until the advent of P.C. Henry Walker Baker; he was a phenomenon. He had, I believe, been a Drill Instructor in H.M. Army, and on his return to civilian life had joined the local Constabulary. A very presentable young man of little more than average height for a policeman, he was very smart and extremely alert, and his physical training was very much reflected in his regulation of the traffic. His arm signals and general movements were precision personified and gave the impression of almost mechanical automation. He was a delight to behold — and I am sure he enjoyed every minute of his time on point duty at Springfield Road corner.

His fame as an entertainer (quite unintentional on his part, I am sure, at the outset) when on point duty grew and spread abroad, and drew large crowds on all sides of the High Street and Springfield Road when he was on duty at Springfield Road during the spring and summer months. He was an extrovert, always full of confidence and always in full control of the situation; if any vehicle driver transgressed or disobeyed his signal, he would approach the vehicle and firmly but courteously reprimand the offender. If no argument ensued he would wave the driver on; if the driver happened to be a young lady, he would more than likely give her a smile and a smart salute. The crowd loved it all. He was a great character.

He was known locally as 'Kruschen' after the then popular brand of Kruschen Salts being sold in the shops at that time. The slogan for this product was something like 'It works like clockwork'. P.C. Baker soon acquired his nickname 'Kruschen'; it was given in good fun and, I am sure, accepted by him in the same vein. He proved to be a good policeman and was soon promoted to higher rank.

Traffic lights now control most corners in Chelmsford — but not Springfield Road corner — and when I am held up in my car at that point I often remember 'Kruschen'.

He became Detective Inspector at Romford, and finally rose to the rank of Chief Inspector, Braintree Division.

He retired from the Police Force in 1960 but died in 1966, enjoying only six years in retirement.

Police Headquarters, I am certain, must have records of his career, but just in case they do not, this is my small memorial to Chelmsford's best remembered policeman.

CHAPTER XX

THE CHANGING FACE

ALTHOUGH a great deal of building and estate development has taken place in and around Chelmsford over the past 50 years the face of the city has not changed much. The building of Caters' Stores has altered the skyline by the Stone Bridge and the Odeon Cinema in Baddow Road has had a similar effect. The most significant change has been in New London Road and the shopping precinct from London Road corner to Market Road and Tindal Square; but these are not changes which can be recognised from the old prints and photographs of Chelmsford as they are, in the main, of High Street. There do not appear to be prints or photographs of the side roads.

The building of the new Police Headquarters in New Street has transformed the corner of Victoria Road where it joins New Street, and the rebuilding of the railway bridge across New Street and the widening of the road there has greatly improved the area between Victoria Road and Marconi Road.

The new Post Office building which is in the process of being built will also change the face of Victoria Road; but all these changes have been made within the last decade.

As far as the centre of the town is concerned — High Street Moulsham Street and Duke Street — the appearance is generally unchanged. New shop fronts have replaced old ones, and additional storeys have been built on many an old shop. A number of old family businesses have disappeared, the sites having been bought up by multiple stores, and such land marks as the Cannon in front of the Shire Hall and the Conduit at Springfield Road corner have been moved to two of the parks.

Many old houses have been demolished between the Baptist Church in London Road and the Council Offices; they were old Victorian-style houses occupied by local businessmen. The offices of the Council are built on part of the site of the Friars — the old monastery of Dominican or Black Friars founded in the middle of the 13th century and demolished soon after the Dissolution in 1537. When the site was excavated a great deal of interesting information was revealed.

The Friars covered a wide area between Moulsham Street and London Road; the site remained undeveloped between the 16th and 19th centuries. New London Road was, however, constructed through the area in the year 1840.

A human burial in a stone coffin was discovered in 1898 in a garden adjoining Friars Walk which was thought to be Roman.

In 1938 the construction of the R.D.C. offices revealed stone foundations which were probably the Priory kitchens, and in 1968 the Chelmsford Archaeological Group located the north and east walls of the Priory at the rear of No. 63 New London Road. There is, however, nothing left to be seen of the Priory or any of its buildings. On the left-hand side of Parkway between New London Road and Moulsham Street, approximately half-way along, the Friars School was erected in 1886 at a cost of £3000 but was demolished in the course of the development of Parkway. The first school which was built on the site was the Royal Free School — the original Grammar School — founded by King Edward VI in the fifth year of his reign, by patent under the great seal of the kingdom, dated the twenty-fourth day of March 1552. This was obtained through the petition of Sir William Petre, Knt., then one of his Majesty's principal secretaries of state, Sir Walter Mildmay, Knt., one of the general supervisors of the Court of Augmentations, Sir Henry Tyrrell, Knt., and Thomas Mildmay Esq., and the inhabitants of Chelmsford and Moulsham, the school to be called by the name of 'the free-grammar school of King Edward the Sixth, for the instruction of youth in grammar learning, under the care and inspection of a schoolmaster and usher'.

It was very liberally endowed by this monarch, with Hills's Chantry in Great Baddow, Stonehouse Chantry in East Tilbury, Cortwyke Marsh in West Tilbury, Plumborough Marsh in Southminster, and Barries and Squire Crofts in Hatfield Peverel. Out of these were paid 40 shillings and eight pence yearly to the poor of Great Baddow for ever, and seven shillings and 10 pence to the Court of Augmentations.

Edward made them a body corporate and politic for ever by the name of 'the Governors of the possessions, revenues, and goods of the free school of King Edward in the parish of Chelmsford'. They have accordingly a large seal of brass, on which is curiously engraven a rose somewhat after the manner of the seal of the privy council. Round the edge of it is the following inscription in capitals:

'Coe.sigill, Gub.Poss.Rev.E.Bonor. Lib. Scho.Fram. Reg. Edri VIth in Chelmsford in con' Essex.'

This seal was found many years ago in one of the streets

of Colchester, and sold; but the purchaser (Philip Morant, the Essex chronicler) generously presented it to the governors of this school.

The four gentlemen who were the chief instruments of the school being erected were appointed primary governors for life; and in their respective families was settled the future government of it. Upon the decease of any of the governors, his heir male was to be chosen; but if there was no such, the governors, or major part of them, were to make a choice of a proper person bearing the estate of a knight, whose family was resident, and whose connections were chiefly in the county. And if it so happened that all the governors died, without male issue, his majesty granted power to the Bishop of London to nominate and appoint four others according to his direction in their room bearing the order of knights. In 1873 a new scheme was approved by the Privy Council, establishing a governing body of 13.

Before any convenient place could be provided, the governors hired a large room for the school at the Friers (now spelt 'Friars'), near the river 'which was before the refectorum, or hall belonging to the monks'. But in the year 1633 the whole roof of this ancient building fell in; this providentially happened in the middle of the day, just as the school was over, and the boys gone to dinner; otherwise all of them must inevitably have perished. However, it prevented its continuance any longer there.

A new school was erected by Sir John Tyrrell, Bart., who was at that time acting governor, on land belonging to the George Inn in Duke Street (formerly Brockhole Street). He likewise purchased a considerable part of the inn itself; this with additions and enlargements he converted into a house for the Headmaster.

The George Inn was on the site of the County Hall in Duke Street, and apparently covered the area as far back as Market Road. The new County Hall is built on this original land and orchards and also a great deal of land adjoining it to the south and west, abutting on the remainder of King Edward's Avenue and Market Road, taking in almost the whole of the square or block abutting on these roads and Duke Street.

The foundations of the present Grammar School in Broomfield Road were laid in 1891.

There were two Charity Schools in the town; one founded 17th August 1713, for 50 boys, and the other, in April 1714,

London Road, opposite the Hospital

The Floods of 1888

Baddow Road Corner

Springfield Road

ier and High Street

The Friars

The Iron Bridge in London Road

for 20 girls. The children were educated in the doctrine of the Church of England, in reading, writing, psalmody, and arithmetic. The girls were further taught household work to fit them for service: taught to make up the linen, and knit the stockings for both schools, and taught to make their own gowns and petticoats. Both schools were cloathed (sic.) once a year. The children were also frequently and publicly examined in the Church catechism. And from both schools many were 'bounded out to proper trades and employments'. Later, the trustees of the school considered it for the good of society, to procure masters for them in husbandry, or to place them out in yearly service.

The school house stood at the north-east corner of the churchyard (the Cathedral) in a lane leading to the Parsonage and to Bishop's Hall. This lane must have run from Rectory Lane, through land now occupied by Marconi Road and Marconi's factory and buildings and through the land covered by the Railway Embankment and Victoria Road and part of Cottage Place to the Churchyard. A long lane in all conscience. But quite a large part of it was apparently taken up by a Workhouse which was erected on part of the same land in 1716; it is described as a large, brick building, being a Workhouse 'for the employment and better maintenance of the poor of this Parish'.

It appears also that this lane may have been part of Church Lane which ran from New Street in an arc to Duke Street along which were built some almshouses, and met Duke Street at the point where the passage from Cottage Place meets Duke Street, i.e. the entrance to Shergold's Printing Works.

The Victoria National School was built on the corner of New Street and Victoria Road (opposite the new Police Station) in 1841 at a cost of £1100 on a site given by Lady Mildmay; this is now used by Marconi's.

CHAPTER XXI

FAREWELL TINDAL SQUARE

THERE IS much more to relate about the Town of Chelmsford, and this could be the subject of another work.

What celebrations, for example, took place in the town on the occasion of the Coronation of George IV in 1821; and on the occasion of Queen Victoria's Jubilee?

There must have been jubilation at Kitchener's conquest of the Sudan, and the end of the Boer War. What did our territorials do in that campaign? What, in fact, did the citizens of Chelmsford do? And the suffragettes? Who was the local Mrs. Pankhurst? What names became household names?

There were a number who achieved fame; mostly among the landed gentry who were in the Services. But what about the ordinary man in the street? In the 1914 War many local men and women were awarded medals for gallantry. There were many others too in the Second World War. Some who had taken an active part in the life of Chelmsford came to an untimely end on one or other of the battlefields of Europe and the Far East, and others lost their lives in the Battle of Britain both in the air and on the ground. Remember too the bombing of Hoffmanns and Marconis, and the unsung heroes of those episodes.

There was the band of men and women who formed the equivalent of the French Resistance Movement, of whom we know little but about whom we should know more.

Many other events have taken place in Chelmsford, the relating of which would be of interest to the present inhabitants, but I hope, however, that this book will give the reader some idea of Chelmsford through the ages.

The impassive countenance of Judge Tindal looks down upon Tindal Square. He has witnessed the changes and will see more. On the whole I think he would approve.

APPENDIX I

ROLL OF HONORARY FREEMEN

4th July, 1903 —
Field-Marshal Sir Henry Evelyn Wood, V.C., G.C.B., G.C.M.G., D.L.

26th November, 1917 —
Frederick Chancellor, J.P., seven times Mayor, including Charter Mayor — Member of Council 1888-1917.

20th November, 1931 —
Walter Cowell, Member of Council 1899-1931.

25th October, 1933 —
Frederick Spalding, J.P., three times mayor — Member of Council 1891-1945.

14th January, 1946 —
Sidney Clifford Taylor, seven times Mayor — Member of Council 1930-1945.

Major General Samuel F. Anderson, of the Army Air Force of the United States of America, Commander Air Forces of the U.S.A. Stationed in Essex during Second World War.

26th May, 1948
George Edmund Barford, Town Clerk 1921-1948.

26th July, 1950 —
The Right Reverend Henry Albert Wilson, D.D., Bishop of Chelmsford 1929-1950.

25th September, 1951 —
Stanley Ling Bolingbroke, Member of Council 1921-1954.

9th October, 1956 —
Arthur Walter Andrews, M.B.E., Member of Council 1926-1960.
Frederick Charles Langton, O.B.E., Member of Council 1937-1962.

28th December, 1966 —
Colonel Sir John A. Ruggles-Brise, Bt., C.B., O.B.E., T.D., H.M. Lieutenant for the County of Essex.

FREEDOM OF ENTRY INTO THE BOROUGH

14th January, 1946 —
The Essex Regiment later extended to the 3rd East Anglian Regiment (16th/44th Foot) and subsequently to the 3rd Battalion Anglian Regiment.

1st March, 1960 —
304 (E.Y.-R.H.A.) Field Regiment, R.A., T.A., and 517 L.A.A. Regiment, R.A. (S. Essex) T.A.

ACKNOWLEDGEMENTS

Miss Spalding for permission to use her Father's photographs.

Mr. R.H.G. Baker for checking details relating to his Father.

Mr. S.J. Burls for information of Hawkes Bros. Ltd.

Mr. Ted Cant for the account of the runaway horse and other items of Chelmsford life.

Mr. P.J. Drury — *Roman Chelmsford* and *Caesaromagus*, in Rodwell and Rowley (Eds.). *Small Towns of Roman Britain, British Archaeological Reports 15,* Oxford 1975 pp. 159-173, and his *Preliminary Report; The Romano-British Settlement at Chelmsford, Essex; Caesaromagus, Essex Archaeology and History* 4 (1973), 3—39.

Mr. G. Hails for his account of the apparition at Springfield Place.

Mr. Jack Hawkes for loaning me photographs of Chelmsford.

Mr. Jack Hickman for information relating to St. Peter's Church.

Mr. Lionel Hills for his memories of shop life in Chelmsford High Street.

Mr. Reg Gibson for his photographs of the floods in Chelmsford in 1888.

The Staffs of Chelmsford District Library, Essex County Library and the Essex Records Office, for their courtesy, assistance and patience and for permission to reproduce a number of the photographs in this book.

Mr. Victor Wilkes and Mr. Harry Ellis for information relating to Trinity Church, Springfield.

BIBLIOGRAPHY

The Essex Review, Vol. IX (1900). Published by Edmund Durrant & Co., Chelmsford.

Chelmsford Planning Survey 1945. Printed by Lawrence Press Ltd., Standard Works, Lawrence Road, London N.15.

Report of the Chelmsford Excavation Committee by Mr. P.J. Drury.

History of Essex by Peter Muilman. Printed and sold by Lionel Hassell (1770).

History of Essex by Thomas Wright. Published by George Virtue, 26 Ivy Lane, London (1831).

People's History of Essex by D.W. Coller. Published by Meggy & Chalk, Chelmsford (1861).

History of Essex by P. Morant. Published and reprinted by Meggy & Chalk, Chelmsford (1816).

The Trade Signs of Essex by Miller Christy. Published by Edmund Durant & Co., Chelmsford (1887).

Chelmsford Official Handbook.

A Guide by Geoffrey Wrayford. Produced by Photo Precision Ltd., St. Ives, Huntingdon.

Narrative of the Deplorable Fire at Chelmsford, March 19th 1808. Published by R.H. Kelhan, Jun., Phoenix Circulating Library, Chelmsford.

In My Young Days by Alderman Frederick Spalding, J.P., c.1930. Chelmsford District Library).

Holy Trinity (Springfield) Magazine, January 1932.

Historical Guide for Visitors by G. Bartrop.

Essex Weekly News, 3rd August 1888 and 21st January 1881.

A True Relation of a Horrid Murder committed upon the person of Thomas Kidderminster at The 'White Horse' Inn in Chelmsford in the month of April 1654. Printed by H. Hills, Blackfriars, London, 1688.

Directory of Essex by William White. Published by Robert Leader, Independent Office, Sheffield (1848).

Survey of 1803 and 1804. Published by Skinner Dyke & Co., Aldersgate Street, London E.C. (January 26th 1805).

Report of Lt. F. Sowrey's shooting down of Zeppelin L.32. Crown Copyright; reproduced by permission of the Controller of Her Majesty's Stationery Office.

119